The Key to Hypnosis

The Key to Hypnosis

A Journey into the World of Hypnosis

Randy J. Hartman, M.A.

Writers Club Press
San Jose New York Lincoln Shanghai

The Key to Hypnosis
A Journey into the World of Hypnosis

Writers Club Press
an imprint of iUniverse.com, Inc.

For information address:
iUniverse.com, Inc.
5220 S 16th, Ste. 200
Lincoln, NE 68512
www.iuniverse.com

ISBN: 0-595-13956-6

Printed in the United States of America

Contents

History of Hypnosis

Even if you are not a bit of a history buff, you hopefully will find this short chapter on the history of hypnosis at least interesting. Since history has little relevance to the here and now, I will attempt to keep this the shortest chapter in the book. When and where hypnosis first began is a point that can be argued to great extent depending on the individual's interpretation of ancient history and documentation.

In the Bible we can find numerous references to the use of something that is believed today to have been hypnosis. In Genesis 2:21, 22; references to hypnosis can be found. The approximate time was said to be about 3000 B.C., and some of the terminology to look for are the various references to sleep temples, the evil eye, and soothsayers. In biblical times hypnosis was thought to have occurred by looking directly into the subject's eyes and speaking in a low steady voice. This is apparently where the terms, "soothsayers" and the "evil eye" must have originated from. The use of sleep temples also lends to the idea of being in trance. People then as well as now tend to confuse being in trance with being asleep. Since the sleep temples were operated by priests and doctors there was probably more credibility to hypnosis then there is now in some parts of the world!

In 1529 a Swiss physician by the name of Paracelsus formed a theory that the stars and their position in the sky exerted a magnetic force that had curative powers. His idea was that magnets placed on the human body where ailments were located would draw the magnetic force from the stars and could influence healing in the human body. It was reported that he met with some success. I guess that serves to further prove the truth to the idea that there is certain magic in just believing that you will get better!

Robert Fudd and Johann Van Helmont provided a new theory about 1626 that provided a different slant to the idea of magnetism as a curative factor. Their idea was that people already had a magnetic force in their body and that by putting two people in the same proximity they could create a magnetic field. Then magnets would be placed on the subjects and moved around the body to generate and facilitate cures. I would be willing to bet that those patients with hemorrhoids were in for a strange experience!

In 1646 a Jesuit priest by the name of Father Kircher that did some hypnotic work with humans and animals. He coined the term, "animal bewitchment" to describe the effects of hypnosis. He found in his work with animals that some could achieve that state of magnetism (hypnotic trance).

Let us not overlook merry old England and how hypnosis shows up in the history there. The legendary wizards and court jesters were reported to have had magical powers of being able to influence people by talking to them. Their use of hypnosis was mostly seen in their story telling, potions, and illusions. Many of the poisons probably evolved from their search for mind-altering chemicals. With the writing styles of the Renaissance era it is quite difficult to discern where truth leaves off and some rather colorful fiction begins.

Magic and hypnosis down through the ages have seemed to go hand in hand. Throughout recorded time reference has been made to magical occurrences or the unexplained, which was assumed to be some sort of magic. The earliest known documents that recorded the prescription for magic to be done was approximately 5 B.C., from the era known as Gracco- Roman Paganism. During this time era magic was referred to as Necromancy. The term Necromancy translates to "Demonic Magic". During this era, magic was used only for evil and damaging purposes. Anyone found guilty of practicing Necromancy was put to death and their body dismembered and burned in separate locations. Another interesting note was that more women than men were suspected and executed for Necromancy. I cannot help but to speculate that possibly this was the first recorded sign of women with PMS problems! This train of thought that all magic was evil carried forward in time to the medieval era when it was recognized that there were good and evil Magicians. The good Magicians were referred to generally as Wizards, and the evil Magicians were referred to as Sorcerers. Here again another distinction is made between males and females. All females that used magic were deemed Sorceresses. It appears that the human race holds on to the mythical belief that women in general command some type of special, evil power. My presupposition is that line of thought is what fostered and still continues to nurture matriarchal societies and organizations. Even the early Greek plays, such as Medea to present day, revere women or bestow upon women some special power of an evil nature.

Both Wizards and Sorcerers alike derived their magic from various sources and their sources would affect what items were of magical value. One example is from approximately 5 B.C. to 7 A.D. Their was special magical value assigned to the nose, fingers and fingernails from crucified people if the corpse was less than twelve hours old. I would speculate that these items were immensely popular after the crucifixion of Christ. In the area we now know as Egypt, there was an extremely special plant that was highly sought after and expensive. This was known as the Mandrake plant. A Eurasian plant, "Mandragora Officinarum", it has purplish flowers. A narcotic was prepared from the root which was called "Mandragoras". Shakespeare used the word in his poetry to describe drowsy syrups. Legend has it that it's top resembles a carrot top with its green leafs. When the Mandrake plant was carefully removed from the ground its roots resemble the human figure when turned upside down. I would assume that the plant's great magical powers probably came from its resemblance to the human body, and secondly it was most likely seen as a male phallic symbol. There seemed to be no limit to the items that would be used in making magic potions and spells.

Another common item used was raw salt. Raw salt added to boiling water would create a tremendous appearance of large foaming bubbles and when added to a type of boiling oil and water it would create traces of colored steam. To create an even more mystical phenomenon some Wizards would pulverize the raw salt into small crystals and with great pomp and ceremony would throw the raw salt into the fire. For even more drama, the Wizards would take pebble size pieces of raw salt and soak them in chicken fat. When this salt was thrown into the fire it would create a thick pummel of smoke. Probably the greatest source of power for these magicians was the power of suggestion, and this still holds true today.

If a person is given a suggestion very convincingly that something will happen to them they will quite often predestine that very thing to occur. People all through recorded time, even today, are quite superstitious and approach the unknown with a fearful curiosity. A good illustration would be the power of the spoken curse and the use of cursed or protective items. Frequently people of that era would hire the services of a Wizard or Sorcerer to put a curse on their enemy. The entrepreneurial thought was that the larger the payment for the curse, the more effective the curse would be. So if the curse failed to meet the expectation of the payee they would be told that they should pay more money for more results. The Wizards and Sorcerers were evidently good business people. I wonder if they ever had special sales like 2 for 1? The use of talismans gained great popularity after the death of Christ. About 1 A.D. the most popular anagrams, or known in those days as "magic squares" on a talisman, were the opening words of the Lord's Prayer in Latin.

Whatever inscription used, it would normally appear as an even number of letters as wide as its height to form the magic square. Not all talismans were done in Latin, different religions and different languages came into use. Also, not all talismans were worn as necklaces. By approximately 45 to 50 A.D. it was fashionable to also have a talisman inscription on a warrior's shield or on a leather cuff. Probably the oldest form of wearing a talisman still seen in our society today is the wearing of a cross on a necklace. The Catholic Church still encourages the use of talismans in the form of symbols; an example might be a necklace with an St Christopher, Virgin Mary, a rosary, etc.

The Irish were no exception as we discuss a fellow by the name of Valentine Greatrakes. He healed his patients by stroking them in a long and continuous manner. His reputation grew rapidly and he went on to work with much of the royalty of his era, because he was thought to have a "magic" touch. He was later known as the "Great Irish Stroker". He commonly would stroke from the shoulder to the wrist many times over. In more recent times we have learned that trance can be easily produced by repetition in most any form, touch, sound, visual, and motion.

The seventeenth century brought even more changes in the field of hypnosis as it continued to slowly evolve. A Jesuit priest by the name of Father Maximilian Hell found his claim to fame from his version of magnetism. He had metal plates fashioned in the frame of about a five-foot man, and then he had these metal covers (plates) laid on top of the naked bodies of his patients. That should have been a chilling, or heavy experience to say the least!

The seventeenth century had many notable people trying to stake their fame with magnetism. The French seemed to be among the front-runners. A man by the name of F.A. Mesmer was trying to sell the idea of animal magnetic force. He believed that the influence of the planets and stars possessed a curative power. His theory was that all humans had a universal fluid that flowed through their bodies, a kind of invisible magnetic fluid that emanated from the stars and was absorbed in the human body. Depending on the position of the stars, the curative impact on the individual would be determined. The only legacy that Mesmer left behind was the term, mesmerized. To be mesmerized was to be held spellbound, as if in trance.

Another Frenchman by the name of Dr. J. Braid had a little different approach to hypnosis. His hypnotic trance was caused by generating subject's eyes through visual fixation. Braid subjects laid down on a table facing up and Braid's head and eyes looked down into their eyes talking to them until he had eye closure. He was on the right track despite his lack of recognition at the time. Later it was found that mental fixation on a particular thought or idea worked equally as well.

Then in the eighteenth century a French neurologist by the name of Dr. J. Charcot at the Nancy School of Medicine attempted to revive the idea of animal magnetism. His new slant on animal magnetism was that he believed only hysterical people could be hypnotized. He claimed that hysterical symptoms without any organic base could be produced and eliminated with the use of hypnosis. Charcot believed that hypnosis was a form of hysteria and considered it a fairly rare occurrence. He went on to discount the idea that hypnosis had any therapeutic value. This notion was not discarded at the Nancy School of Medicine until after Charcot's death.

Many people will be left unmentioned in this account of the history of hypnosis, but we could not overlook the pioneer of psychoanalysis, Dr Sigmund Freud. Freud actually studied under Charcot for a period in Nancy, France. He abandoned his use of hypnosis because he felt that a very deep state of hypnosis was required for any therapeutic cure, and consequently felt that very few patients would benefit from the use of hypnosis. Freud never rejected the validity of hypnosis directly, but with his tremendous prestige his followers took this to mean that hypnosis had no value and never considered incorporating hypnosis in their practice.

In the United States Dr. Clark Hull was credited for developing the "Standardized" method of hypnotic induction. Dr Hull taught at the University of Michigan for many years. He subscribed to the idea that one hypnotic induction would work for everyone! Hull even went on to have this standard hypnotic induction put on phonograph records to be distributed for sale to therapists nationwide.

One of Dr. Hull's young medical students, Milton Erickson is credited for bring hypnosis to its present form. Erickson went on to develop the "Utilization" technique with hypnosis. The utilization technique has the therapist using whatever the patient brings to them, resistance for resistance, cooperation for cooperation. Another fascinating point about Milton Erickson was his use of analogies and metaphors as curative factors. He was truly a master of his craft and gained worldwide recognition for his work. Dr. Erickson seemed to possess an innate ability and insight as suggested by the many books written about him and his work. Currently the Ericksonian approach to hypnotherapy is the most widely accepted form of hypnotherapy in the United States.

All of these premises and by-products of magic/hypnosis still exist today in one form or another in the world around us. Magic in its positive form is now used for entertainment, but unfortunately the negative side of magic is still seen in occult practices and in manipulation of people. Hypnosis has now evolved to a medical form that has positive indications for people. On the negative side hypnosis is still widely used for entertainment which in turn continues to give the use of hypnosis a negative implication. Consequently people continue to shun hypnosis as a medical intervention.

In summation, I find it fascinating that the art of magic /hypnosis has survived over the centuries to our present day society. What I find appalling is that society still continues to wrongfully assign some evil meaning to hypnosis.

Properties of Hypnosis

Hypnosis has been defined and explained several ways by the professionals in the field. We will take a look at six different explanations of hypnosis, and then I will offer my version of a definition of hypnosis.

Paulo believed that hypnosis was a partial sleep or a special excitation of certain cerebral regions and relative depressions of the other cerebral zones of the brain. His ideas were interesting, but not provable with scientific research. With some subjects there seems to be a more active abstracting ability, and the sensory system becomes more acute. This information coupled with the idea of being able to by-pass the conscious mind does give this theory some credence.

Sigmund Freud had written about hypnosis and inferred that hypnosis; trance in particular, was a transference phenomenon. He contented that to engage in hypnosis with a patient was the sign of a love relationship. He went on to explain hypnosis as an erotic relationship between the hypnotist and the subject. We have long come to accept that the hypnotist needs not to have an emotional or physical relationship with the patient to do successful trance work. Some people have speculated that Freud could not clearly distinguish when his patients were, or were not in trance because of his cocaine addiction. Truth or fiction, I really don't know, but it sounds plausible.

Dr. Clark Hull who was a noted physician and teacher made the statement; "All sciences alike have descended from magic and superstition, but none has been so slow as hypnosis in shaking off the evil associations of its origin". I find this a very true statement, and we have the entertainment industry to thank in part for the negative image that hypnosis has been saddled with.

Musad Ansari, PhD, colleague and master of hypnotherapy in all respects defined hypnosis in his book titled "Modern Hypnosis", as a particular altered state of selective hyper suggestibility brought about in an individual by the use of a combination of relaxation, fixation of attention, and suggestion. This appears to be the easier definition to accept as it embodies the principles of trance work. By having the subject relax and focus, they become open to the suggestion, and the suggestion in whatever form becomes the curative factor. There are more elegant ways to describe hypnosis, but I prefer simplicity to the more confusing technical jargon.

Dr. Milton Erickson was an M.D. Clinical Hypnotherapist, and the frontrunner for change in hypnosis in the twentieth century. He wrote about hypnosis for patients as their selective perception, a process in which the patient chooses to see only what is relevant to their task and blocks everything else out. With this statement I believe Erickson was pointing out the patient's enhanced ability to focus while in trance. With that enhanced focus coupled with suggestions, changes and shifts can occur for the individual.

Our old friend the Webster Dictionary defines hypnosis as an artificially induced passive state in which there is increased amenability and response to suggestions and commands. So much for the dictionary! This is a rather vague look at what hypnosis is about and what happens. None of these descriptions are totally alike; they seem to look at hypnosis and the trance state from different views.

When anyone asks me what hypnosis is, my standard reply is simply: "It is an altered state of awareness". When doing trance work we are helping our subjects move into an altered state of awareness while they continue to be aware of what is going on around them. Hypnosis and trance, really one in the same, is difficult to define exactly as we all tend to interpret our experiences of the same thing differently. So for a clear understanding in a simple form, it is easier to approach hypnosis as an altered state of awareness. What the person chooses to do with that altered state of awareness can also vary greatly. On a daily basis we all move in and out of trance when we focus our entire attention on a subject and fail to recognize other things going on around us. Most of us can relate to this by remembering times when we were so engrossed in a book or TV show that we didn't hear someone trying to speak to us, or driving from point A to point B and not remember anything we saw on the trip.

Misconceptions abound in our society about the subject of hypnosis. Over the years I have heard numerous and varied misconceptions on the subject of hypnosis. Probably the most common misconception I have heard over the years is that hypnosis is a form of sleep. Sleep doesn't really enter into the picture. On a rare occasion a person in trance will convert to a state of fugue and not remember in the conscious state what was said. We also must consider the fact that the misconception is further fostered because the word "hypnosis" comes from the Greek word for sleep. Ivan Petrovich Pavlov was a Russian physiologist who worked with conditioned reflexes in dogs; he asserted that there was a connection between hypnosis and sleep known as cortical inhibition.

Some people labor under the misconception that only weak-minded people are more hypnotizable than intelligent people. This is completely untrue, and the fact is that intelligent people are more easily hypnotized. The best possible hypnotic subjects are those people of average or above average intelligence. They are generally seen as possessing a stronger motivation and a higher ability to concentrate. In the past I have been asked what segment of our society is more hypnotizable, my response has always been that I stand by the idea that anyone that can be socialized can be hypnotized. Depending on the knowledge and skill of the hypnotist, practically anyone can be hypnotized.

Another interesting myth is that the hypnotist should have a dominant personality. This thought echoes the idea that the hypnotist should have a strong, dynamic, and commanding personality. It was assumed then that men supposedly have dominant personalities and would be better hypnotists than women, this is totally false. There are a large number of women who are outstanding hypnotists in our country. The act of going into trance is done totally by the subject, not the hypnotist and this disproves the need for dominance.

The danger of not being able to come out of trance is another example of the exaggerations that abound. Any occurrence of a subject not coming out of trance would be a rare incident. Even then, a trained hypnotherapist would have little or no problem overcoming the resistance and easily bring the subject immediately up from trance. Later in this book we will talk about various methods for arousing a subject from trance.

Some people express a fear that if they go into trance they will reveal intimate secrets about themselves and be out of control. There is no basis for their fear, as a person in trance will always be in control of themselves and their behavior. In trance a person will not do anything that they don't want to do. There are people that are predisposed to certain illegal behaviors that could be influenced by an unscrupulous hypnotist to commit a criminal or antisocial act. Unfortunately, there are a small number of hypnotists that use hypnosis in an unscrupulous manner to take advantage of their patients.

Some people have suggested that hypnosis is harmful, even dangerous. Hypnosis could possibly be harmful if the trance was applied by an untrained or inexperienced person. There is a possibility that they could take the subject in trance back into a painful memory or damaging experience without the benefit of intervention. The only danger is the mismanagement, not the hypnosis itself. A countless number of people have been hypnotized repeatedly without the slightest sign of any problems. It has been my experience that patients with numerous inductions always report feeling refreshed and relieved of tension.

Possibly the strongest statement I can make about hypnosis is that the curative possibilities are only limited by the skill of the hypnotherapist and the cooperation of the patient. While stop smoking and smoking cessation programs seem to be identified with hypnosis, the uses for hypnosis seem to be endless. A few of the multitude of uses could be: weight control, insomnia, drug habits, alcoholism, migraine headaches, pain management, self esteem, PTSD, age regression, habit control and phobias; the list goes on indefinitely.

To give a better understanding of hypnosis and the phenomenon of trance I will take this opportunity to contrast the differences between being asleep and being in a hypnotic trance. We will address six specific differences between sleep and trance. There are more differences observed in the two, but the six differences illustrate with clarity the point being made.

1. The conscious mind is bypassed in the state of natural sleep. When the subject is in the hypnotized state, both. the conscious and unconscious minds are combined and work together, or the conscious mind can be bypassed and the unconscious mind is addressed directly.

2. During trance the subject can respond to commands and suggestions, physically and verbally. While in natural sleep

the subject does not respond to verbally or physically commands or suggestions.

3. When the subject is under the influence of hypnosis the knee jerk (Patellar Reflex) is present and active as if the subject were fully conscious. During periods of natural sleep this reflex is absent. The Patellar Reflex has been proven to only be available during a subject's conscious state, in trance or otherwise.

4. During a state of natural sleep the subject's muscles become flaccid and remain limp, except for involuntary muscle spasms. When a subject is under the influence of hypnosis they can exert voluntary muscle rigidity such as walking, grasping and moving objects.

5. During a subject's normal state of sleep their cardiac and respiratory system reduces its overall activity by 35-50%. In contrast, while the subject is under the influence of hypnosis their cardiac and respiratory system will normally remain close to the same level of functioning as when the subject is fully conscious. This gives way to the possibility of working with patients who take cardio medication or have pacemakers.

6. Now here's a tip for weight loss patients. When a subject is in hypnotic trance their basal rate of metabolism remains near the same rate as when the subject is fully awake as opposed to sleep. When a subject is asleep their basal rate of metabolism decreases ten to fifteen percent. By using a hypnotic trance, a hypnotic suggestion might be for the subject's metabolism to remain the same 24 hours a day to aid in weight loss.

As I stated earlier, there are other differences between natural sleep and the hypnotic trance, but the six examples cited above are possibly the most important ones to bear in mind. Usually this information is quite adequate to put the first time hypnotic subject's mind at rest and feeling informed. Most hypnotic subjects will respond better if they feel informed on the subject of trance before subjecting themselves to hypnosis.

Another important issue to look at is a question usually posed by possible hypnosis patients: Who is really most susceptible to hypnosis? I still must stand by my statement earlier that anyone who can be socialized can be hypnotized. We will take a brief look at this question from a few different angles, first by age:

1. Age seven and below, poor subjects. During this period in the life cycle a person's ability to concentrate and stay focused has yet to be fully developed.

2. Age seven to fourteen years old, good subjects. The child's ability to concentrate and focus is steadily improving with age.

3. Age fourteen to twenty-one years old, excellent subjects! I imagine this may come as a surprise to you if you have ever raised teenagers. Their ability to stay focused and concentrate is at its peak during this time in the life cycle.

4. Age twenty to seventy years old, generally declines with age. In general, our ability to stay focused and concentrate on just one issue at a time diminishes with age. Some subjects will be affected more severally.

5. Age seventy-five years old and older, generally regarded as poor subjects. Just as with item four, the concentration and focus become even more impaired with the passing of time. Overall, age should not be regarded as a significant issue when working with hypnotic subjects. The well-trained hypnotist can easily overcome most of the problems associated with reduced concentration and focus.

As these chapters continue it will become apparent and very clear how these subjects with a reduced ability to concentrate and focus can be easily hypnotized.

On the gender issue, there really seems to be no difference between men and women as hypnotic subjects. For quite some time there was speculation that women were better hypnotic subjects, but the results of testing have proven men and women as equal. Interesting enough, there are more women than men that present for hypnotic treatment overall. This is probably because women are more adventurous and willing to take risks for self-improvement.

Occupations are an important point to address here briefly. Those people that engage in very mundane work or routine jobs such as factory workers, clerks, etc are usually quite susceptible to hypnosis. Other segments of our population that is very susceptible to hypnosis are military personnel, religious people, and domestic help. By the nature of their work and interests they tend to follow orders well. Also included in this category are writers, artists, and other people with a strong abstracting ability. Those people that would be difficult subjects would be people who are accustomed to giving orders, and people who are highly analytical and scientific minded.

The personality of the subject can also be a consideration for the hypnotist. There has been research done that indicates there is a relationship between personality types and susceptibility to hypnosis. The research indicates that introverts are slightly more susceptible than extroverts. Senile persons, paranoids, and imbeciles are very difficult, nearly impossible subjects to work with. Their ability to concentrate and focus is extremely poor, if not non-existent. Usually neurotics are not a problem to hypnotize, but I must issue a warning at this point about personality types/mental illness. Until the hypnotherapist has gained some further detailed training and experience I would caution them to not work with this group alone. Seek supervision!

Linguistics Explained

Everything we do in this world around us is dependent on linguistics in one form or another. Even our perception and understanding of linguistics will affect our attitude and behavior towards society. How we choose to see, hear, and feel the world around us gives us linguistic content that shapes our emotional responses. Linguistics is simply communication, spoken or symbolic.

To linguistically reframe information is to reintroduce known information to an individual in a no threatening manner that frames the information in a positive context. To clarify that idea I would offer that well-worn cliché, "Every dark cloud has a silver lining". We as human beings seem to have a tendency to dwell on negative information rather than positive information.

On a daily basis we are bombarded with negatives from the media, friends, family, and the job. If we reframe the negative situations to positive situations they automatically become more tolerable and easier to deal with. Two examples of reframing the linguistic content would be:

Complaint: I feel horrible because my wife always criticizes the way I dress.

Response: She must really think enough of you to be concerned about your appearance.

Complaint: My wife takes forever to make a decision on anything.

Response: It sounds as though she is very careful about making her decisions. Since she chose you, that should speak well of her decision making skills!

These are only two examples of many possibilities for linguistically reframing negative thoughts to more positive ones.

Metaphors are also a vehicle for changing the linguistic content and meaning. A wonderful example would be a very old Chinese Taoist describing a farmer in a poor country village. He was considered very well to do because he owned a horse that he used for plowing and transportation. One day his horse ran away. All his neighbors exclaimed how terrible this was, but the farmer simply said, "Maybe". A few days later the horse returned and brought two wild horses with it. The neighbors all rejoiced at his good fortune, but the farmer just said, "Maybe". The next day the farmer's son tried to ride one of the farmer's wild horses, and the horse threw him and broke his leg. The neighbors all offered their sympathy for his misfortune, but the farmer again said, "Maybe" the next week the conscription officers came to the village to take young men for the Army. They rejected the farmer's son because of his broken leg. When the neighbors told him how lucky he was, the farmer replied, "Maybe".

The meaning any event has depends upon the "frame" in which we perceive it. When we change the frame, we change the meaning. Having two wild horses is a good thing until it is seen in the context of the son's broken leg. The broken leg seems to be bad in the context of peaceful village life, but in the context of conscription and war, it suddenly becomes good. Reframing changes the frame in which a person perceives events in order to change the meaning. Accordingly, when the meaning changes, the individual's responses and behaviors also change.

Reframing a person's behavior is not a con job. What makes a reframe work is that it adheres to the well-formed conditions of a particular individual's needs. It is not a deceptive device; it is actually accurate. The best reframes done are the ones which are as valid a way of looking at the world as the way the individual sees things now. Reframing doesn't necessarily need to be more valid, but they really cannot be less valid.

When the father says, "My daughter is just too stubborn" and you say, "Aren't you proud that she can say no to men with bad intentions?" That is a very valid way of looking at that situation. At another time and place, the father would actually look at it that way and be proud of her, but he did not think about it until it was brought up. You cannot reframe anything to anything else. It has to be something that fits that individual's experience. Saying to that father, "You should like your daughter being stubborn because that means she is a liberated woman" probably is not going to work with him. You have to find a valid set of perceptions in terms of that particular individual's model of the world.

What reframing does is to say "Look, this external thing occurs and it elicits this response in you, so you assume that you know what the meaning is." If you thought about it this other way, then you would have a different response. Being able to think about things in a variety of ways builds a spectrum of understanding. None of these ways are really true. They are simply statements about an individual's understanding.

Linguistics is a large portion of what doing trance work is all about. What you say and how you say it can strongly influence what impact the hypnotic work may have. It is extremely vital to listen closely to what the individual is saying, or more precisely, what they are not saying. Most people tend to globalize in their statements about their problems. There are many ways this is commonly communicated by the individual.

Simple deletion is one way. This is where some persona event or object has been left out. The best example I could offer would be, "I'm really very unhappy with Ralph". What goes unsaid in this statement is what exactly about Ralph is it that makes the person unhappy. Once a person can assimilate what specifically the problem is, then they can focus on a resolution.

Another communication problem often seen is a lack of referential index. This is quite similar to a deletion as a person or object goes unspecified. An example of that could be, "They never believe me". What goes unspecified is who are they. In some cases I have found that there is not a specific "they", but rather the individuals did not believe in themselves, so they presupposed no one else would believe them.

A comparative deletion is when a specific person or point of reference is deleted when making a comparison. A good example of this would be, "It's better if I don't go to school". What goes unspecified here is "who" is it better for, or compared to what? These generalizations need to be reduced to specifics before forward movement can occur.

Sometimes unspecified verbs become another way of generalizing, as they are not explicit as to the action that needs to be taken. A good example of this would be, "Fred really frustrates me". What needs to become clear is how specifically Fred frustrates the individual.

Another way these linguistic problems reveal themselves is through nominalizations. This is seen when an ongoing process is presented in a way which may distort its meaning. The example offered is, "I can't stand his insensitivity". The verb that is nominal is insensitivity; just processing this quite often can build insight for the individual about whom or what specifically is insensitive.

A different slant on linguistics is verbal manipulation in communication. This usually is seen as a means of eliciting some promised positive behavior change in an individual. There appear to be two approaches. The first approach is a "bind". This generally forces a person to make a win or lose decision, and normally is an uncomfortable situation for the individual. A radical example would be, "Confess or be shot".

A more positive approach would be a double bind that provides for a win-win situation. A double bind is more likely to produce a positive outcome. A good example would be, "Do you want to eat supper at 5:30pm or 6pm?". What ever time the individual chooses, supper will still be accomplished. Any time you can deal with an individual in positive linguistic terms, you can easily expect forward positive movement.

There are numerous volumes of information available on the subject of linguistics, but in this chapter I have endeavored to deal with only a. select few linguistic models. I would recommend as a general rule of thumb that linguistics incorporated with trance work be kept specific and fairly simple for the maximum pay value.

Listening to what individuals say and the direction of their eye movement will help us understand just exactly how people access the world around them. Once these fundamentals are understood we adjust our choice of language to better meet their model of the world, thereby solidly connecting with others by speaking their language. The Neureo Linguistic Programming (NLP) has devised the following information to "read" people by watching their eyes and listening to their choice of words. First we will take a look at eye accessing to determine what mode a person dominantly operates in. For sake of simplicity I have broken it down in to three categories: visual, auditory and kinesthetic. To find out which mode a person primarily operates in, start by watching their eye movement. For individuals that are primarily visual, their eyes will tend to dart up and either left or right, depending on what is being said at the time. If the eyes dart up and to the right they are visually constructing images. If their eyes go up and to the left they are remembering.

Another interesting thought to hold onto is the concept of talking to the different hemispheres of the brain. J. E. Bogan had developed the "split brain theory" in the past, and this can now be incorporated into doing trance work. Bogan's concept was that right handed people process logical information via their right ear to the left hemisphere of the brain and emotional based information via the left ear to the right hemisphere of the brain. In doing trance work the thought here would be that you could cast your voice to the left or right ear depending on what information you are providing that is logically or emotionally based. For the relatively new hypnotherapist I would recommend not allowing yourself to get caught up in the idea that you have to follow this idea to the letter, as in the beginning it could become a great and unnecessary source of frustration. Over time and with experience this theory can be incorporated in your performance of trance work to enhance the information you are sharing with your patient.

Suggestibility Tests

Every now and then you are bound to have a subject ask you to prove to them that they are susceptible to hypnosis, or you may feel the need to find out how susceptible a subject is before doing trance work with them. This is where these suggestibility tests come into play. With these simple tests in the waking state you can evaluate their hypnotizibility for doing trance work very readily.

The approach to doing these tests can be done differently depending on the subject. An authoritarian style or permissive approach can be used, depending on the subject's "model of the world." Since I am from the Ericksonian school of thought on hypnosis, in good conscience I could never recommend the authoritarian approach. If a subject is so resistive to trance that I would need to use the authoritarian approach, I need to stop and find out what the problem really is before proceeding.

The first suggestibility test is known as Chevreul's Pendulum test. This test was devised by a French chemist by the name of Chevreul. This test validates the thought that involuntary muscle movement takes place in the human body. This activity is known as "ideomotor activity". The mind controls the muscle movement, thus the muscles respond involuntarily to thoughts, ideas, and feelings.

To construct Chevreul's pendulum, use a thread, chain, or string about ten inches long. To this string you can attach a key, paperclip, or ball. The next step is to draw a circle about eight inches in diameter on a piece of paper, then draw two lines though the circle, from top to bottom and. left to right so they cross in the center of the circle. Then label the left side with the word "true", and the right side labeled "false. Next label the top of the circle with the words "Maybe", and the bottom "Don't know".

Now have the subject sit down in front of the circle on the paper and instruct the subject to hold the string with their dominant hand so the object on the end of the string is just slightly above the paper. This test can be done in a standing or sitting position. In either case ensure that the subject is not resting their arm on their body to hinder the movement of the pendulum. Instruct the subject to concentrate and the ball will move spontaneously by just thinking about the answer. The ball may move left, right, up, down or in a circle. At this time you can ask the subject a question and their answer will cause the ball to move with involuntary muscle movement so miniscule that the muscle movement cannot be detected, but the ball will move accordingly. The larger the swing of the pendulum, the more susceptible the individual is. It is rumored but unknown for sure that this is how the Ouija board came about.

Another simple test that is used is called the Arms Rising and Falling Test. This is where you ask the subject to stand upright with their feet together with their back against a wall and their arms hanging loosely at their side. Now have the subject stretch their arms straight out in front of them at shoulder height and close their eyes. Begin now explaining to the subject that one hand is palm up, holding a very heavy telephone book, and the other hand is sideways with the thumb upwards. To his thumb is attached a balloon that is tugging and pulling his thumb gently upwards as the phone book in the other hand is growing even heavier and forcing his hand downwards. Continue repeating this for a few minutes and note how the hands start moving according to the suggestions given. Then ask the subject to open his eyes and take notice of the difference between the hands. This test can be done with groups or with individuals. It is a fairly good test of an individual's susceptibility to suggestions.

The Postural Sway Test is something you might have seen done at a party in the past, but still considered a test of hypnotic suggestibility. The backward postural sway test has the subject standing upright with both feet together and eyes closed. The hypnotist standing behind with arms outwards and finger tips on his shoulders. The hypnotist starts to gently pull the subject backwards very slowly, and telling the subject that he can feel a force also pulling him backwards. When the subject starts to lose their balance the hypnotist catches him. The postural sway test determines the individual's suggestibility if they will comply with request of the hypnotist. There are several variations of this procedure, including the forward postural sway test, but hardly worth any mention at this time.

The Eyeball Roll Test we will discuss now deals more with physical properties that physiological ones. During this test ask the subject to close their eyes and roll their eyes upward and hold their eyes in that position while asking the subject to try and open their eyes, meanwhile reinforcing verbally that they can open their eyes. This really seems to border on deception, as it is nearly physically impossible to open your eyelids while you have your eyes rolled upwards. The true power of suggestion is not really demonstrated with this test. The Eye Roll Test can be better labeled a "parlor trick", rather than a hypnotic suggestibility test.

Another suggestibility test that falls in the category of "parlor tricks" is the Hand Clasp Test. For this test you ask the subject to remove any rings from their fingers before starting, or otherwise this test can become needlessly painful. Now instruct the subject to interlace the fingers of both hands. At this point have the subject tighten their finger grip, telling them: "Squeeze your fingers tighter and tighter, making them as tight together as possible, tighter yet, making your fingers so tight that they feel glued together, notice how they feel, glued together, now relax and notice your fingers won't come apart. Now they are slowly separating from one another".

What has happened is that temporary muscle rigidity had set into the subject's fingers, as if they were glued together. It is important to say the last sentence quite quickly before the muscle rigidity in the fingers lets go.

It is merely an illusion that the fingers were glued together, as stated earlier, just another parlor trick.

If the hypnotherapist has took adequate time to build rapport with the subject, none of these suggestibility tests are needed. Stage hypnotists tend to use hypnotic suggestibility tests to locate easy hypnotic subjects in their audiences. This is another good opportunity for me to plead my case against using hypnosis for entertainment. Using hypnosis as entertainment and parlor tricks only serves to continue to discredit the therapeutic use of hypnosis for the general public.

Preparation for Trance Induction

There are a few basic issues we must examine in preparation for starting a trance induction. Over time and with experience you will become exposed to a wide variety of challenges while doing trance work. These issues we will discuss here are mainly what I call the garden variety of issues that I am presupposing that you may be faced with in the future. If in the future you are doing trance work and feel that the situation is geing out of your control, relax and realize that the situation was never in your control in the first place! It is essential to remember that as a hypnotherapist you are the guide for your patient, but the patient will normally do only as much as they choose to do regardless of how you struggle with them. With that thought in mind we will go on to look at the six basic causes of resistance to dehypnotization.

1. Your hypnotic subject may have negative feelings towards the hypnotist. The hostility may be acted out in a passive aggressive manner by not coming back up from trance when asked to.

2. The individual may be trying to test the ability of the hypnotist to bring them back up from trance. Here again there may be some negative feelings acted out by a passive aggressive personality.

3. The hypnotic subject may be unwilling to carry out a certain post hypnotic suggestion in the conscious state. This should not be a problem if you and the subject had agreed upon the positive outcome of the trance work.

4. The individual just may not be willing to relinquish the state of trance they are in. Some subjects have reported the state of trance to be better than any known drug to create that feeling of euphoria.

5. Some hypnotic subjects have a very difficult life situation to face and would rather remain safely in trance. Trance can be a beautiful source of escape for those individuals involved in a dysfunctional lifestyle. It can provide temporarily the peace and harmony they are seeking.

6. Infrequently a hypnotic subject could be only partially de-hypnotized and can lapse back into a deep trance spontaneously, even deeper than the previous trance. This usually occurs when the subject is brought back up from trance to quickly, or not verbally engaged immediately after coming back up from trance.

Now that I have offered you six possible reasons for a hypnotic subject's resisting de-hypnotization, I would like to share with you six different methods of arousal from trance in the event just counting the individual back up from trance seems ineffective.

1. Ask the subject while they are in trance to speak and tell you why they will not relinquish trance. It is best to not struggle with the patient, but rather seek a verbal explanation of the lack of cooperation.

2. Inform the hypnotic subject that if he will not come back to the conscious state that he will be left alone. Most people do not like the idea of being left alone outside of their environment. While the idea seems passive, it often is highly effective.

3. Several texts recommend that you blow sharply on the closed eyes of the hypnotic subject. Personally I do not recommend this procedure as I am very much against doing anything that makes the trance experience a negative one.

4. The individual just may not be willing to relinquish the state of trance. It has been reported that some subjects feel trance is better than any drug they ever tried.

5. Inform the subject that if he does not awaken, he will not be allowed to experience the pleasure of trance again. This is a passive threat that does work extremely well with resistive subjects, as long as you have made sure that trance was a pleasant experience.

6. Another option from various text books on the subject instruct you to tell the hypnotic subject that his face will be washed with a cold wash cloth unless he awakens! This is not a good choice; the subject could become very upset and even possibly do you physical harm.

Of these options I would highly recommend number five over the other options for arousing a resistive subject. The use of a passive threat is very effective and does not set up any negative conflict between the hypnotist and the subject. As a backup option I would suggest using number one. It is simple enough to ask the subject in trance to tell you what is interfering with them returning to consciousness.

To also prepare you for doing trance work, we need to have an awareness of what to expect the hypnotized individual to report of their trance experience. I have compiled a list of the more common psychological signs that individuals report after being exposed to trance work. They are:

1. A strong disinclination to want to move spontaneously or even apply effort. Trance subjects often relate that they feel

they could move, but just choose not to so they can continue to enjoy the wonderful feelings of trance.

2.   The feelings of peacefulness and calmness. For many hyp-
     notic subjects this is probably the first time in many years
     that they have experienced any sense of peace and calmness
     in their life.

3.   It is very common for hypnotic subjects to report feelings of
     heaviness in the limbs during their trance experience. It is
     explained as a comfortable sense of heaviness in their arms
     and legs that does not generate any cause for alarm.

4.   A general sensation of numbness and tingling over their
     entire body. This seems to occur due to the increased
     relaxation and blood flow throughout the body to parts
     that have been previously deprived due to stress and low
     blood flow.

5.   A good many hypnotic subjects also report a sense of
     being relieved and in better command of their senses. All
     outside interference is shut down and the individual has a
     superior focus.

6.   Some hypnotic subjects report the feelings of lightheaden-
     ness when they first enter trance. This disappears quickly
     during the trance experience.

7.   Some hypnotic subjects will experience an interesting
     phenomenon such as an out of body experience without
     suggestion by the hypnotist. This feeling of detachment
     from the body is best described as feeling ultra-light during
     trance. You can anticipate this happening very rarely.

8.   Another wonderful phenomena that occurs is time distortion.
     Underestimating the time that has elapsed is quite common.
     It is as if time has almost stood still. This time distortion
     affects both the hypnotic subject and the hypnotist. A large
     wall clock located in your office can be an asset for you.

9. The majority of hypnotic subjects will express a disinclination to be awakened from the pleasant feelings of trance. With the stress in our society and work-a-day world hypnotic trance provides a wonderful relief.

As stated before, these are the more typical responses you can anticipate from hypnotic subjects, but are not limited to the above listed nine items. It all centers largely around the hypnotic subject's model of the world. By always debriefing your hypnotic subject after trance, it provides you with the information to facilitate an even better trance experience in the future for the individual.

When doing trance work there are four observable physical changes that nearly all hypnotic subjects display. By observing these physical changes you can validate that the hypnotic subject is moving into trance. These will be:

1. The hypnotic subject's breathing will slow down. Usually the subject's breathing pattern will be seen as upper chest breathing, and as they start to slip into trance their breathing pattern will move to the lower chest and upper stomach area.

2. Facial muscles will relax and the skin will smooth out as they go into a deep state of trance.

3. With some clients you will observe eye twitching and also observe their eyeballs moving under their eyelids. This is a natural function of the client experiencing visual stimulation in trance.

4. Those subjects that have a high stress lifestyle could display facial or finger twitching as they first enter trance.

As you are preparing to start trance work it is good to remember that it is important for the hypnotic subject that you validate their experience as it is happening. This is where we tie in the above listed observable physical changes as you see them occur. Along with observable we need to include the non-observable feelings that we presuppose the hypnotic subject is experiencing. This serves to continue to turn the subject's focus inwards to validate what you are saying. The typical non-observable we will deal with here are such things as "The flow of your blood has gradually slowed down", "Your heart rate has slowed down to a comfortable rate", "You are feeling warm and comfortable".

To use these observable and non-observable in the early stage of the trance it most probably would sound like:

"As you continue to relax and go deeper into trance you can notice that your breathing has slowed down to even a more comfortable rate, and also notice that the muscles throughout your body have started to relax and let go, also taking the time to notice that your heart rate has slowed down to a very comfortable rate and enjoying that warm and comfortable feeling as it continues to move throughout your body and perhaps the flow of your blood has gradually slowed down to a comfortable rate".

Another idea for consideration of doing trance work is using simple conjunctions in your hypnotic patter. The flow of your hypnotic patter should never be marked with a period, but is simply a never-ending sentence using: "and", "but", "maybe", etc. Open-ended questions are good for continuing to turn the hypnotic subject's thoughts inward to increase their focus. Close-ended questions during the hypnotic induction should be avoided and reserved for the pending intervention. The best advice I can offer is to relax, go with your patter and attempt to keep your transitions smooth and appropriate as possible, bearing in mind it is all right to have pauses during hypnotic induction.

As we continue to prepare for the hypnotic induction we need to look more closely at what to say, and how to say it. What to say for an initial induction might be like the following example:

"Now I would like you to make yourself comfortable. Now take two very slow and deep breaths, filling your lungs all the way up, and now slowly letting your breath out until you empty your lungs. Now let your breathing return to normal and focus on the sound of my voice. As you continue to relax and let the beautiful feelings continue to grow, you can go deeper, allow your mind to be inactive and let every thing else float on by, noticing how your breathing has slowed down and the flow of blood has also slowed down to very comfortable rate".

On how to say it, allow your voice to remain steady with an even flow. It is not necessary to lower your voice. One extremely important note here is that you should continue to pace the subject's breathing by verbally marking key words with the inflection of your voice. A good example of pacing and marking would be using the word DEEPER in your hypnotic patter. Every time you use the word DEEPER, say it on the subject's exhale and pause before going on. You can use any variety of words to do this, just remembering to say the word on the subject's exhale. As you continue to do that throughout the trance, the subject will go more easily into trance and remain at a good working level. A simple point that works very effectively, but can be easily overlooked by the novice in the field.

Basic Trance
Induction Techniques

There are an immeasurable number of trance inductions that can be used to induce trance. The inductions I will address here are very basic in nature, no fire and smoke type of razzle-dazzle involved. When working with hypnotic subjects I believe it is most important to utilize whatever fits their model of the world. These three basic inductions should be suitable for most individuals as they are best described as user friendly.

The first basic induction is utilizing visual imagery to start the induction. You start by simply asking the hypnotic subject to visualize their favorite animal or object. Then instruct the subject to imagine that they can become that image. As they start focusing on that image just continue your hypnotic patter to deepen the trance. You can expect that the subject will voluntarily give up that image as they go deeper in trance. If your subject is not a very visual person then you might need to switch to a more appropriate induction to meet their model of the world.

This next basic induction is known as the "Star Technique". Here again, this is presupposing that your hypnotic subject is visually oriented. You can start by asking the subject to visualize a star in their mind. Tell them to imagine that the star is suspended far away in the distance. Now slowly talk the client through the idea that the star is moving closer towards him, slowly and safely. Once the star is close, ask the subject to reverse the star and have the star starting to move away. Now tell the subject that when the star fades out of sight he will be in a deep comfortable trance. With this technique you could substitute the star with a circle, square, etc, and expect the same results.

My favorite of the basic inductions is the eye fixation technique. I always recommend to my students that they first try this induction at the beginning of their training. To use the eye fixation technique you should start by asking the hypnotic subject to assume a comfortable position and fix their gaze at an object above eye level in the room. Ask the subject to take two very long deep breaths and exhale slowly. Then have the subject resume normal breathing. Start your hypnotic patter and go on to verify their trance experience for them as we had discussed in the previous chapter. When the subject's eyes close a light trance has been achieved. In some rare instances you may have a subject go into trance with eyes remaining open, not moving or blinking. If this occurs ask the subject to close their eyes so their eyeballs do not start drying out and become irritated. One of the reasons I recommend this basic induction is because you have the subject's eye closure to validate the beginning of a light trance. The next few pages are a sample script to give you a better idea of what this induction would sound like, and for your trance use it if you care to use the script. In this script please note that I have included a "Special Place" in this hypnotic patter. Using a special place is optional, but I have found it very useful. Later in this book I will elaborate on the usefulness of a special place. This script is double spaced to make it more readable as you start to practice trance inductions.

Basic Script

Assume a comfortable position now and let your eyes focus on that object on the wall while now taking a deep breath. Fill your lungs all the way up now and slowly exhale. Once again, filling your lungs up completely and then exhaling slowly now. Allow your breathing to return to normal. Notice the warm and comfortable feeling starting to spread all over your body as you continue to relax and just enjoy that very warm and comfortable feeling as it continues to spread over your entire body. When your eyelids grow heavy and tired they can gently slide closed when you feel the time is right. Just relax and allow that warm and comfortable feeling to continue to grow and become more comfortable. Just slowly letting go, allowing yourself to go deeper into that wonderful state of relaxation. Allowing yourself to let go and enjoy those wonderful feelings as they just continue to grow and move slowly throughout your body. Just enjoy the peace and serenity as you relax even more. Letting go and moving one level deeper, moving deeper at a pace that is comfortable for you. Not to fast, not to slow, just very comfortable for you. Knowing the whole while that you are safe and secure, very much in control of your situation. As thoughts come to your mind, they can drift on bye. The only thing that is important is hearing the sound of my voice. The sound of my voice can go with you, the sound of my voice can give you the comfort and relaxation that so richly deserve as you continue to slowly drift downwards into trance. There may even be nice odors to smell, enjoy the colors even take a second to turn up the brightness of the colors enjoy the things you have surrounded yourself with. Knowing that in your special place you are safe and secure and very comfortable as you keep that special place in your mind. You can allow yourself to go deeper as you see yourself in that special place you can also see yourself holding a pretty (color) balloon, this pretty balloon is filled with helium, tied to a string that is attached to your finger, what a pretty balloon. You can see it there, tied to your index finger, tugging and pulling at your finger as it playfully tugs at your finger, it will slowly lift it in a playful and wonderful way, such a pretty balloon admiring it. Knowing that you can gradually slip one level deeper into trance, so wonderfully deep, enjoying your special place as you go one level deeper.

After you take the hypnotic subject into trance the first time, all subsequent trance work will go faster. This happens because the subject now knows where to go when trance work begins. The hypnotic subject is now familiar with the wonderful feelings and their special place. After the first trance you can then employ the "Piggyback" technique. To use the "Piggyback" method is as simple as having the subject close their eyes and think of their last trance experience as you verbally reinforce the experience and continue to deepen the trance. The more sophisticated methods of induction are done by implementing confusion. There are a variety of confusion techniques an individual can employ to induce trance. This is done primarily by setting up a state of confusion in the hypnotic subject's mind. There is a story about Dr. Milton Erickson that best exemplifies using as confusion technique.

He had a patient referred to him that had seen numerous other Hypnotherapists who could not get her into a state of trance. So Erickson started the induction by utilizing confusion with the subject. He simply started with telling the subject that he could not hypnotize her, but he would hypnotize her arm! This did set up an appropriate amount of confusion for Erickson to successfully accomplish trance work with her. The subject's normal pattern of thinking was interrupted by confusion. It has been said that interruption is an established pattern of being.

The first method I will discuss is the "Double Induction" technique. This consists of having two hypnotists applying a trance induction simultaneously while using opposing information. It is recommended that you have a hypnotist on each side of the subject at the beginning. Each hypnotist talks at the same time, but using opposing information, such as; one hypnotist would be talking about becoming heavier and going deeper while the other hypnotist is talking about feeling lighter and going higher. When the subject cocks his head towards one hypnotist the other hypnotist ceases to speak while the other continues with the trance work.

A simpler method to consider would be to have music or sound effects playing just below the noise level in the room. With your hypnotic patter and the low music in the room the subject's mind will normally dart from your voice to the music and continue back and forth until he gives up and focuses on your voice. This method appears more reasonable to use than the double induction technique. In most clinical situations there is little need to employ a confusion technique. More commonly the confusion inductions are helpful with those subjects that are highly analytical. I normally refer to these subjects as my "emotionally constipated" patients. They are somewhat more difficult to get into trance because they appear to live outside their "feelings" self, but once in trance just proceed like any other hypnotic subject.

On the following page will be a sample script for the "Piggyback Induction". This type of induction is excellent to use with subjects who have already been exposed to previous trance work. These subjects have acquired the knowledge of what it feels like to be in trance, so they know exactly where they are going as they recall all the feelings of previous trance work.

At this point I would like to encourage you to find a volunteer and attempt your first trance induction. Go for it!

Piggyback Induction

This induction method is for clients who have already experienced hypnotic trance. This procedure has the client revivifying their last hypnotic experience.

Ask the client to assume a comfortable position and start with their eyes closed. Read the following script; As you continue to relax with your eyes closed, listening to the sound of my voice, you may begin to remember those experiences of hypnosis that you have had before, how it felt to listen to that voice speaking to you. Remembering that sound and the words as you begin to drift down, that feeling in your hands or legs or arms, that feeling of relaxation perhaps, and what you thought as you begin to enter that deep state of trance, the sensations and images, the alterations in awareness, as your conscious mind became more and more comfortable, and your unconscious mind, assumed more and more responsibility for guiding and directing thoughts and responses, remembering where you were, in what position, what you did, what was said to you, how you felt as you learned to allow that trance to continue, and even now, as you continue to re-experience the memory of that event, and to allow those feelings to become a part of your experience now, I would like you to have the opportunity to enjoy allowing that trance to continue as you drift deeper and deeper, and my voice drifts with you, to become a part of your experience.

(Continue with an intervention)

Confusion Induction Script

This induction would be good for working with individuals who are highly intellectual people/critical thinkers.

Ask the client to take three long, slow deep breaths and then settle back comfortably with their eyes closed. Then begin with the following script; Now, before you begin, I should say how glad I am to be working with you today, instead of a dull-witted mind, the kind you might find, in the gutter some place arguing with everyone, mad at the world, because when I see them, they keep shifting around, scratching itches, never getting comfortable, thinking they know it all, and no one can tell them what to do, not even to help them and they refuse to learn anything that might get them to climb out of that place and take care of themselves, so it is nice to know that anyone with your intelligence can easily learn how to drift into trance, so you can sit there, in that chair, here, while you try to be aware of the exact meaning of the words you hear and all the changes that occur there in your thoughts, sensations, or awareness as I speak here, or you can forget to try to make the effort it takes to pay close attention to everything that happens, or does not happen in your experience, as you listen to me and also to your own thoughts, or to your sensations that change over time, or stay the same, in an arm or an ear, and your legs or fingers, and what about the thoughts, and the variety of images that speak to your mind's eye as I speak to your mind, and what you speak to yourself speaks for itself as you try to search and find that things may seem to be one thing, but turn out to be another, because two and two are four, but two can also mean also, and no two are alike, it all belongs to you and to your own ability to relax, those two ears too, and to begin to know, that you really don't know what means yes and what means no, here, though you may try to guess where you're going to go, you don't know that there is no real way to know how to let go while holding on and to recognize that there is nothing you need to try to know, to do, or not do, because everything you do allows you to recognize that I can say many different things and there is no need for you to make the effort it takes to try to make the effort to pay close attention to each thing I say, or don't say, because there was a time when the effort to train the mind to stay on track was not worth the trip that led the mind back to that time of peaceful, calm awareness, of effortless letting go, and knowing that you don't need to try to hear, or to understand what I might say later on here, the conscious mind, can go anywhere it wishes, while I continue to talk, and your conscious mind continues to hear, the way you overhear a conversation, you don't even need to do anything at all, it all belongs to you, as you begin to hear, the way you do, here and now, with your eyes closed, comfortable, listen to that voice or sound in the background of the mind.

Trance Depth

Once you have an individual in trance, what happens next? In this chapter we will take a look at how to deepen the trance state and be able to recognize what level of trance your hypnotic subject is in.

The deepening procedures differ from one hypnotist to another, depending on their preference. Here I will discuss five very basic procedures for deepening the hypnotic trance. The first deepening procedure is simply utilizing silence. Explain to your subject while he is in trance that you will be silent for the next two minutes, and to sit there and enjoy the wonderful feelings of trance as he goes deeper. The silence and enjoyment of trance will allow the hypnotic subject to spontaneously deepen the trance.

The second method will be to anchor to a word, telling the hypnotic subject that they will go at least one level deeper every time they hear the word. It is important here to remember to verbally mark the word on the exhale of the hypnotic subject. By using a specific word you will set a sense of expectancy on the part of your subject as they wait to hear the designated word several times during the trance session. The example I will offer would sound like: "Every time you hear the word "DEEPER" from the sound of my voice, you will go one level deeper into trance". Remembering to use the word on the subject's exhale several times throughout the trance work.

The third method would be taking your hypnotic subject on an escalator ride. This is done by having the subject in trance visualize themselves riding down an escalator one floor at a time. Ensure that they see their self-stepping onto a well lit, slow moving escalator as they descend deeper and deeper one floor at a time. Some people do not like the idea of riding an escalator, so beware of the hypnotic subject's model of the world.

Method number four has you actually touching the hypnotic subject. To accomplish this deepening technique you need to stand behind your hypnotic subject who is already in trance and tell him you are going to put your hands on their shoulders. Press down gently on the shoulders as you count slowly from one to five. With each number you say, press a little firmer on the shoulders. This is also generally known as stuffing someone into trance! Be aware of your hypnotic subject's model of the world, not all subjects are going to want to be touched.

The fifth method I have dubbed the yo-yo technique. In. reality it is known as Vogt's Fractionation Method. It is essentially described as hypnotizing and de-hypnotizing the subject several times during the same session. Each time the hypnotic subject is told they will go deeper in trance each time they are hypnotized. Under most any circumstance a hypnotic subject will tend to automatically go deeper into trance with each induction, so this way it is all combined in one session. This method can provide a fast means to move your subject to a state of somnambulism.

Now that we have talked about ways to deepen the hypnotic trance, we need to clearly distinguish the different levels of trance and what you can expect to accomplish at these different levels. First we will examine the six levels of trance.

DEPTH	OBJECTIVE SYMPTOMS
HYPNOIDAL	Pupils of the eyes decrease in size and eyes redden with a glazed distant look. Blinking and drooping of the eyes. Physical relaxation begins along with eye closure.
LIGHT	Eyelids will not open easily. Extremity Catalepsy is limited at this depth. All muscle activity is reduced. Pulse and breathing slows down to a relaxed rate.
MEDIUM	Total physical relaxation occurs. Deeper and slower breathing. Reduced motor activity. No sensation of pain. All sounds fade away. Extremity catalepsy occurs.
SOMNAMBULISM	Artificial amnesia can be installed and anesthesia of body parts or total body anesthesia. Eyes can be opened by suggestion of the hypnotist. The hypnotist voice may start to fade in

	and out. Memory increases about 65% without suggestion. Can feel detached from body. Positive and negative hallucinations can be inducted in all senses.
PLENARY STATE	Suppression of all physical actions. Complete feeling of a euphoric nature. Overall catatonia of the body and total anesthesia without any hypnotic suggestion.
HYPNOSLEEP	A true amnesia occurs as there is a loss of conscious awareness

Trance Depth Scale

In this hypnotic depth scale no numerical value has been assigned to any occurrence, as every individual will experience the feelings/responses in slightly different orders. The ideal "working depth" of trance is somnambulism. The following chart will better illustrate what type of intervention is best accomplished at what level of trance.

Hypnoidal

This is a good working state for psychoanalysis, or just interviewing the anxious subject. The Hypnoidal state also represents partial physical relaxation that can settle a client down so they can focus better on their issues. Also at this level, uncomplicated suggestions can be given.

Light Depth

At the light depth there is increased physical relaxation, normally accompanied with eye closure. This is not a good state for hypnotic work. In this state ego strengthening is the best possible intervention to be accomplished.

Medium Depth

In the medium state you can remove the sensation of feelings from arms, legs, etc. At this level would be a good place to introduce a posthypnotic suggestion or post-hypnotic analgesia. This would also be a good state to do all your desensitization work with your subject.

Somnambulism

As stated earlier, I recommend this level of trance for doing most of your hypnotic work. This level of trance is ideal for introduction of posthypnotic suggestions and post- hypnotic anesthesia. Also at this level you can easily accomplish age regression or something as simple as hypno analytic work.

For working with any hypnotic subject on an outpatient basis this is most ideal.

Plenary State (Coma)

Since this is a very deep state it is ideal for working with individuals who suffer from intractable pain from cancer or arthritis. Remembering that anesthesia naturally occurs at this level also makes it ideal for performing surgical procedures and child birthing. To reach this trance state takes some additional hypnotic work and it will be discussed later in this chapter.

Hypnosleep

Hypnosleep is an extremely powerful anesthesia. This level of trance is good for the removal of preoperative tension and anxiety and is also quite good for recalling deeply buried traumatic events in the past. Since Hypnosleep involves attaching hypnosis to sleep, we will also deal with this subject as a separate procedure later in this chapter.

To employ the use of the coma state you must take the trance work we already discussed to another level deeper to achieve this depth. The coma state brings with it a total feeling of euphoria. In the coma state, nothing bothers or disturbs the individual; the hypnotic subject is even able to give himself a complete anesthesia. Although the subject will not respond either verbally or nonverbally in the coma state, he has complete awareness. When questioned after being in the coma state, the subject can relate everything that had occurred while they were in the coma state. To accomplish the depth of the coma state, first you need to get the subject into trance and down to the level of somnambulism to start. Use the elevator deepening technique to move the subject down to the "basement of relaxation". The following sample script is offered as an example:

"I know how relaxed you must be now, but we will go even deeper now to a whole new and better state of relaxation. In your mind I want you to picture yourself stepping into an elevator. Now as the elevator starts down I want you to know you can relax twice as much as you did before we reach the next floor relaxing twice as much as we move towards the basement of relaxation". (repeat this until you have talked the subject down three floors, and then once more to the basement of relaxation).

Once this is accomplished, without a suggestion proceed to give the hypnotic subject the following two tests to validate the coma state:

1. Ask the hypnotic subject to open his eyes. If the individual is truly in a coma state there will be absolutely no movement of the eyeballs or eyelids.

2. Perform a test of limb catalepsy without giving the hypnotic subject a suggestion. Move the individual's leg or arm to any position and it should remain in that position without any movement or muscle tremor.

If your hypnotic subject has successfully completed these two tests they are in the coma state. Once the subject is in the coma state he cannot be aroused by the more standard methods. In the coma state the individual is usually reluctant to give up that wonderful feeling of euphoria. The best way to arouse the person from the coma state is to passively threaten to deprive him of these wonderful feelings if he does not come out of trance. With that possibility in mind, the individual will find it easy to return to consciousness.

For the deepest possible level of trance there is Hypnosleep. With Hypnosleep you will. be actually attaching a state of hypnosis to a state of natural sleep. You can expect this procedure to be time consuming and probably test your patience. The following procedure is recommended to achieve Hypnosleep:

1. Count the number of respirations per minute while the individual is fully awake. The average person will have around sixteen to eighteen respirations per minute in a resting conscious state. Now put your hypnotic subject into trance and give a posthypnotic sleep suggestion to take effect after he is back out of trance.

2. Bring the hypnotic subject back out of trance and give the signal for him to lapse into a natural state of sleep. Now patiently wait and count the respirations of the subject until he has achieved six or seven respirations per minute. If the individual is breathing too fast, you must wait until he is in a more sound state of sleep.

3. What we are attempting to do is to bypass the subject's critical faculty without awakening him. You must approach your hypnotic subject very gently and carefully so as not to awaken them. In a soft and confidant whisper, start with saying: "This is (Your name) speaking, you can hear me but you will not wake up". Repeat this and everything you say at least five times. It is necessary repeat yourself at least five

times to be able to penetrate the subconscious mind in sleep. Then continue verifying Hypnosleep by saying the following at least five times: "I will know you can hear me when your left index finger which I am touching begins to rise". To accomplish this you first need to place your finger gently on top of the subject's left index finger so you can feel any muscle movement. Any muscle movement you detect will be very slight. Once this is accomplished you can proceed with the intervention.

4. When you have concluded with Hypnosleep your next step is to remove the hypnotic state and return the individual to a state of natural sleep. When Hypnosleep has been induced in your office you need to tell the subject that he will now sleep for five minutes and awaken refreshed and relaxed. If hypnosleep is induced at night simply tell the subject that he will sleep throughout the night and in the morning awaken refreshed and alert.

Interventions
With Hypnosis

Interventions are really what brings people in to see you for hypnotic work. In this chapter we will examine some of the more common interventions with hypnosis. The general public will undoubtedly bring a wide array of problems they want resolution to. There is no way I can possibly offer a solution for all the problems you will be presented with. There are numerous volumes written on this subject and several more volumes yet to be penned. Probably the best advice I can offer when you are faced with a new and unusual problem is to consult with a veteran in the field and keep your creativity wide open for possibilities. Creativity in hypnosis can serve you well if you remember to work within your hypnotic subject's model of the world. The more you practice the art of hypnosis, the more the possibilities will seem to unfold before your eyes, so remain a possibility thinker! If the individual can accept it in their model of the world, then it can become quite possible.

In this chapter we will talk about hypnotic suggestions, age regression, future pacing, and dealing directly with the subconscious parts of the mind. Many of these interventions are Neuero Linguistic Programming (NLP) in nature and modified for use in trance. As we proceed in this chapter you will note that I will state that the intervention can be used in or out of trance. It is much like having a double-edged sword in your therapeutic toolbox. My preference has been to use these in trance. To use the comparison of glue, to use these interventions out of trance is like using regular glue, while using the interventions in trance is much like using super glue for increased "sticking" power.

Before any successful intervention can take place you and your subject must first know what the problem is. This sounds simple, but it truly is more complicated than it appears as many individuals may not be entirely clear about just exactly what their problems are and their priority of importance. Because of this possibility I would like to offer the following NLP procedure known as the "Outcome Frame" for use in the initial session to clarify their problem(s). Start by asking the following questions:

Blame Frame

What's wrong?

Why do you have this problem?

How does this problem stop you from doing what you want?
Whose fault is it that you have this problem?

When was the worst time you experienced this problem?

What we are doing here is getting through all the normal "blaming" that needs to take place so the individual can get it out of their system and take another look at their problem in a healthier manner. Human nature in our society dictates that by nature we must go through the blaming frame as almost habit. To move forward we must now ask the following questions:

Outcome Frame

What do you really want?

How will you know when you have it?

When do you want it?

What el-se in your life will improve?

What resources do you have to help you with it?

How can you utilize those resources?

What are you going to begin doing to get what you want?

Many times when people are confronted with these types of questions they often respond with "I don't know". You cannot accept this for an answer as the individual is usually reluctant to look inside for answers and assume responsibility for their problems. Try to keep the individual working in the positive and identify their internal and external resources. Also ensure that their desired outcome is realistic and achievable. Some people have a tendency to set grandiose and unrealistic expectations for theirselves and consequently pre-destine theirselves to failure before they ever start. By sorting the chafe from the wheat in the beginning by using the Outcome Frame, you will save valuable time for you and your subject. Different subjects will offer you different problems at different levels. Some people will offer up a secondary problem to see how you can handle it before they will admit to their primary problem. The wise use of the Outcome Frame will help you cut through all of this nonsense in the beginning.

The use of post-hypnotic suggestions and suggestions is a broadly used form of intervention. The use of suggestions is virtually without limit for hypnotic subjects. Posthypnotic suggestions are commands that are suppose to take place on cue after the individual is out of trance. Suggestions are more commonly used in trance for deepening and to offer the subject better choices in lieu of previous unacceptable behavior or thought patterns. By using commands instead of suggestions you will be setting up conflict with the subject. Most individuals resent commands whether they are in or out of trance. Suggestions in their passive form allows the individual to make choices within their model of the world. A common standard in the field of hypnosis for suggestions are the "Five Laws of Suggestion". Now we will examine and explain the five laws of suggestion.

1. The Law of Reversed Effect: With this law the harder one wills oneself to do something, the less likely they are to succeed, It has been found that the imagination is much stronger and more powerful than will power. When you phrase a suggestion the hypnotist should use all the principles of "imagination power" rather than rely on "will power".

2. The Law of Dominant Effect: This law indicates that a strong emotion tends to replace a weaker emotion. Love and anger seem to be the strongest of all emotions. To achieve the greatest possible results from any suggestion, if possible, attach the suggestion to an emotion that bypasses any other emotion in the individuals mind.

3. The Law of Temporal Precedence: Considering that all other things being equal, when two antagonistic suggestions are given, the one that is given first will take precedence over the second suggestion. This is good to remember if you should slip and use antagonistic suggestions.

4. The Law of Depth of Precedence: When two conflicting suggestions are given, the subject will carry out the suggestion associated with the greatest depth of trance. This law is basically saying that the deeper in trance the suggestion is given, the more likely it will be carried out.

5. The Law of Impressional Precedence: This law suggests that all things being equal, of two opposing suggestions, the suggestion installed most strongly through factors other than trance depth will take precedence over the others. This law is basically a repeat of number two. It is important to also bear in mind that not all suggestions can be easily attached to emotions.

To summarize these five laws of suggestions I would offer the idea that the most complex suggestion given at the deepest level will take precedence over all other suggestions. To really increase the effectiveness of posthypnotic suggestions I would recommend you build a higher order of complexity. To build this higher order of complexity you need to first formulate your basic suggestion and repeat it three times during trance. Each time you repeat the suggestion you need to add new information to it to build the complexity. The following will be an example to illustrate this point:

1st suggestion: You will find it interesting that you will no longer have an urge to smoke cigarettes.

2nd suggestion: You will find it interesting that you will no longer have an urge to smoke cigarettes and you will find the taste and smell of cigarettes disgusting.

3rd suggestion: You will find it interesting that you will no longer have an urge to smoke cigarettes and you will find the taste and smell of cigarettes disgusting and this will make you feel nauseated and ill.

It is important to take note that with each suggestion something is added to build the complexity. The subconscious mind is very concrete and deals with information better in small chunks over time. This way the subconscious has sufficient time to assimilate the information.

To install posthypnotic suggestions with your trance subject you need to start by describing in detail "what" will trigger the reaction, and also describe in detail "what" the reaction will be. "What the reaction will be" is going to be your post-hypnotic suggestion. At the level of somnambulism reinforce the suggestion three or more times, building the complexity of the suggestion each time. If feasible, test the posthypnotic suggestion before the client departs from the hypnotic sessions you can also reinforce the posthypnotic suggestion in future sessions if indicated.

It would also be a good point to state that you should tackle only one issue per trance. If you are working with an individual for weight loss, nail biting and fear of snakes, you need to use three separate trances to address all three issues. For the maximum effectiveness of your posthypnotic suggestions it is also recommended that you limit yourself to one posthypnotic suggestion per trance. You may want to take a moment to reflect back on. The "Five Laws of Suggestion" that were addressed earlier in this chapter.

Using a hypnotic "Key" with your subject for future sessions should be an ideal consideration for progressing trance work. This procedure works the same as installing a post-hypnotic suggestion. First, you can use a word(s) or phrase(s) as the trigger. It is highly recommended that you use the same key word for all of your hypnotic subjects to avoid confusion. Install the key word and reinforce using:

1. The "key word" will help you slip into a comfortable trance, easily and quickly.
2. Only when you hear it from "the sound of my voice".
3. Reinforce at least three times during trance.
4. After trance, test the "key" by immediately triggering the key word and re-inducing trance.

It is important to remember to attach the key word to only the sound of your voice. This is an important safety feature for your hypnotic subject. If this safety feature is not used, the subject could be driving or some other high risk task and hear the "key" word in his environment and start to immediately go into trance. This safety feature is too important to disregard!

Aversion therapy is another way of employing a posthypnotic suggestion. This is accomplished by building the complexity of a post-hypnotic suggestion as we have discussed earlier. Aversion therapy can be used with a wide number of situations. The field of addictions is possibly the most used area for aversion therapy. For the hard core, long standing addict, the success rate will probably be less than fifty percent. With the hardcore addict it often becomes a test of wills. The safety feature built into this procedure is that the suggestion will be voided by the subconscious if the situation becomes life threatening. Regardless of what you might say or do, the individual's subconscious is always in control of the situation, and especially strong if the information does not meet their model of the world.

Now we will discuss a wonderfully simple procedure known as separating the conscious from the subconscious. To separate these two entities probably sounds like an awesome thing to attempt to do, but hang in there because it really is simple. For a moment I would like you to reflect back to the basic induction script I offered in an earlier chapter, back to the part where you asked the subject to create a "Special Place" in their mind. This is where we can use this special place for the conscious mind to go while we deal with the boss, the subconscious mind.

The example I offer would sound something like this while the subject is at the level of somnambulism: As you continue to relax and go deeper, I want your conscious mind to return to your special place and relax and enjoy relaxing more while I talk with your subconscious mind. (Pause and ask the following question) Am I now talking to (Name) subconscious mind? Raise your left index finger once for yes and twice for no".

Now that you have accessed the subconscious mind and shut down the conscious process you are ready to move on with the needed intervention. You can establish communication with the hypnotic subject by asking them to speak or installing ideomoter signaling. To install the ideomoter signaling, ask the subject to raise their index finger once for yes or twice for no, or use a simple nod or shaking of the head. My recommendation is usually to ask the hypnotic subject to speak while they are in trance. With limited dialogue from the subject you have the opportunity to know first hand what is going on with your subject. If all the responses you need are no more than yes or no, then ideomoter signaling would be most appropriate. It is all basically a matter of using what ever seems to fit the hypnotic subject's model of the world at the time.

Remembering the past sometimes is essential so the individual can move forward in the present. Hypermenesis is often an overlooked phenomenon of trance work. Hypermenesis is the term for magnified memory recall in trance. The individual's memory recall increases sixty five percent just being in trance at the level of somnambulism. With this phenomenon, age regression may not even be needed.

Age regression is a most misunderstood hypnotic phenomenon among the public.

Two different situations can be contrasted with examining the past. One is age regression and the other is revivification. Age regression is where the subject looks back into the past only as an observer of events. Revivification is when the subject withdraws into themselves and tries to recreate the world of their past. The personality of the regressed subject will be changed and they will think and behave as they did at that point in time. To achieve either state of trance it is important to begin going into the past from the hypnotic state of Somnambulism. If time allows the first attempt at regression should be to a very happy and positive time in their life. On occasion while doing regression the hypnotist can become a stranger to the subject and making all conversation and rapport more difficult. The problem is resolved by making the hypnotist into someone known and trusted to the subject at that time in their life.

This is why it is so important to take a detailed background history.

To take an individual back into the past you must first take them down into trance to the state of somnambulism. Then instruct the subject that they will be floating back in time in five or ten year increments. Taking the subject back in time in incrementsis usually comfortable, all the while reminding them that they can see the past float on by, but they will not stop to visit. Ideally it is good to have the subject float back in time just past the target event and then move them forward to the desired event.

Then use hypnoalaysis talk to the subject and elicit the needed information.

Weight loss is another popular issue with hypnosis. It seems that the general public is always looking for a quick miracle cure for being obese. For most people weight loss is a life long battle, losing weight for six months and gaining it all back in two months. In America today weight loss has turned into a multi-billion dollar industry. It has been my experience that the weight loss issue is really "Pandora's Box". It would be extremely rare to treat an individual whose only real problem is weight loss. Usually there are a variety of issues that seem to be driving the weight problem. These other sub-issues must be uncovered and addressed before any truly effective weight loss program can be implemented. Over eaters are not necessarily gluttons, they are often people who are searching for security. This search takes them back to the time when oral satisfaction represented complete security, when mother fed and took care of them. They eat, and continue to eat, because eating gives them the sense of security, which allays a fear lurking below the level of conscious awareness.

With every weight loss case the fear has a different cause, but it is really the same kind of fear and all such fears are similar. This does not mean that the same treatment will work for every person, nor does it mean that hypnosis should be used simply to give every person a suggestion. A hypnotic diet without the removal of the fear may provide only temporary help. Excessive overweight is often caused by strong emotional conflicts which can be resolved by an approach utilizing hypnoanalysis.

Every neurotic problem has a beginning, and obesity is most often a neurotic problem. In most cases once the individual has gained clear insight into their problem, the appropriate changes start taking place and the weight comes off in a healthy manner. We must also bear in mind that there are undoubtedly people who don't want help with their problems. They profess a desire for help and even seem to seek it, but when the help is offered, they refuse to take it. I am of the opinion that this unwillingness to get well is part of their illness another way to look at this problem is that the individual is attempting to commit suicide in a slow manner. Before accepting anyone for treatment of obesity they should be checked by a medical doctor for any existing pathological conditions.

On the following pages you will find various scripts that can be used for treating different problems that your subjects may present with. The important thing here to remember is to just take a deep breath and simply proceed with the script, reading it slowly and continue to pace the subject's breathing pattern.

Balloon Technique

This technique can be used for intervention with various problems; i.e. grieving, stop smoking and habit control. During the assessment interview note the significant points that stop a person from achieving the desired change.

Take the client into trance, deepen to Somnambulism. Ask the client to go to their special place, a place that they feel comfortable, safe and secure. Build the intensity of their special place.

This is a sample scrip for stop smoking and the significant points to overcome are as an example; (1) Craving tobacco (2) Light headiness (3) Unspecified anxiety.

Sample Script

Enjoying your special place, knowing that you are comfortable and safe there, Notice the colors about your special place, how very nice, notice all the other things about your special place, the sights, the sounds, the colors, no one else can be in your special place unless you allow them, what a wonderful place to be, so comfortable and safe in your special place, so wonderful-, notice how you feel, comfortable and safe, enjoying your special place. Notice that in your (left) (right) hand you are holding three balloons, three of the ugliest balloons you have ever seen in your life. These ugly balloons look so out of place in your special place, these are such ugly repulsive colors on these balloons, the first balloon has the words, "Craving Tobacco" written on the side, the words are clear and easy to read, the second ugly balloon has the words "Light Headiness" clearly printed on the side. The third ugly balloon has the word "Anxiety" clearly on the side, there you stand with these three very ugly balloons with the words, "Craving Tobacco", "Light heartiness" and "Anxiety" wrote on the balloons. These ugly balloons certainly do not belong in your special place as you observe these ugly balloons with the words on them, you realize even more that they don't belong in your special, beautiful place. When you are ready, you can release these ugly balloons and watch them slowly float up and away, moving slowly out of sight. As the balloons start to fade away, so does the words printed on them, remembering briefly that the words were "Craving Tobacco", "Light headiness" and "Anxiety". Watch them slowly disappear from sight (Pause). Now you can see yourself in your special place, free of the ugly balloons, free of the tobacco craving, light headiness and anxiety, seeing yourself in your special place as a nonsmoker. Noticing how you look now, how wonderful, notice how very wonderful you feel, feeling so proud of yourself now that you are a nonsmoker, how wonderful to be so rightfully proud of yourself, seeing yourself as a non smoker, experiencing how it feel's to be a non smoker, how wonderful. Continue to relax, perhaps moving even one level deeper, enjoying the experience of being a nonsmoker. (Bring client out of trance and process the experience).

The View of Life

The purpose of this exercise is to provide the individual and the therapist a better understanding of the individual and how they are oriented to life. This should provide significant insight for the individual into how they are in dealing with life and problems.

Begin with taking the client down into trance; medium stage would be appropriate to start. Tell the client the following story:

Script

Now I want you to picture yourself approaching a wall, this wall can be any size, shape, color or texture that you want it to be. Take time now to notice the wall. What does it look like? What does it feel like? Is it hot or cold? Does it have a smell? Now you must cross the wall, you can use anything you want to cross to the other side, the only thing you can't do is blow up the wall. Now you find yourself in a nice forest setting, as you stroll down through the forest you can notice the tall trees and pretty flowers along the way. Now you find yourself coming up to a river, you pause there to look at it. This can be a flow of water anywhere, because you have seen this flow of water before. Now is the time for you to prepare for your journey up stream to the source of the water. You can take any thing you want with you on your journey to the source. Now you have started your journey up stream in search of the source. Now you are approaching the source of the water. Now that you are at the source of the water, I want you to closely examine it. Now its time for you to go back down stream. You slowly turn away from the source and start your journey back. Along the way you notice a bit of a beach in front of you, I want you to stop there briefly now that you are on the beach doing whatever you want to do. Now its time for you to leave the beach and continue back down stream. As you continue back down stream you see the place where you started. Now you step back into the forest and walk back down the path until you see the wall again. Now you are standing in front of the wall again, examine it closely now. As before, you need to go to the other side of the wall now by any means you choose. Now you are standing on the other side of the wall where your journeys first begin.

Now bring the client back up from trance. Check their orientation to ensure that they are out of trance. Explain the following meanings to them about what they encountered on their journey:

The first wall represents your natural wall of defenses to others in the world around you.

The forest represents nothing, a transition from the wall to the water.

The river/flow of water. This represents your flow of life as you are experiencing it presently.

The source of the river/flow of water represents your very life essence. Your source of energy, motivation, etc.

What you did on the beach represents your ability to play.

The second wall represents your present defenses in life.

Now have the client describe their journey in detail and assist them in understanding the significant points of their journey.

Meeting the Inner Child

The purpose of this exercise is to assist the client in getting in touch with their inner child. This in itself should generate insight for the client as to what their present needs might be, and lend additional insight into lifelong behaviors.

Take client down in trance, medium state to start.

Tell the client the following story pacing their breathing throughout trance.

Script

Think back now to when you were 7 or 8 years old, (pause) now picture in your mind the place you lived when you were that age (pause). Now imagine that you are standing outside that very place looking at it, now walk around to the door you mainly used when you were a child, slowly now open the door and walk in, notice the sights, sounds and smells that were familiar to you (pause), continue to walk to the room where you used to feel the most secure and comfortable in. there as that 7 or 8 year old child, notice what you are doing, how were you dressed? (pause) Now tell the child the most important/valuable information that he or she can use in their coming years now that you are an adult and have lived those years (pause). Go ahead now and speak to the child and tell them what they need to know (pause). Now give the child a hug before you leave, if you can't hug the child, and then just say good-bye (pause). Now turn and walk back out the same way you came in. Continue to walk to the location where you first viewed the place where you lived. (Terminate trance, ensuring that you empower the client's memory).

You can expect this experience to be very impactful and profound for some clients. You need to ask your clients to explain their experience in detail to you from start to finish. This experience should help build insight and possibly identify issues to be resolved in the future.

Pain Management

In the traditional medical community hypnosis is best known for its use in pain management. The use of hypnosis for pain management can be extremely effective if used in the proper context. Probably the greatest misunderstanding among the general public is the thought that pain can be eliminated permanently with hypnosis. That is why I have chosen to entitle this chapter as pain management rather than pain control. With the use of hypnosis an individual can learn to effectively manage their pain or be assisted by a hypnotist is managing their pain.

My preference has always been to empower the individual with the knowledge and skills they need to successfully manage their pain without assistance. Not all individuals have the emotional peace or self-confidence in the beginning to learn and self-administer these skills. As with all things in the world of hypnosis, we must first identify and operate within their model of the world.

In this short chapter we will discuss six different approaches to pain management. Other approaches are possible, but we will continue to deal with the basics in our look at pain management with hypnosis.

Amnesia

This approach is designed to help the subject "forget" about the pain via distraction. During this process do not use the word, pain", and do not remind them of the problem. With this technique we are teaching the subject to disassociate from the pain. A few good examples would be to tell the subject to "take your mind on a shopping trip to the mall" or to "leave the pain here and move to other side of the room". Another possibility would be to confuse the subject by moving the pain to a healthy area of the body so the pain can be dealt with more efficiently. Along this line I am reminded of a story I heard about Dr. Milton Erickson. It was reported that he taught pain disassociation to one of his patients by having her understand that whenever she experienced pain she would also know that there was a tiger under her bed, so she must lay still so as not to awaken the tiger!

When you devise the form of disassociation for the subject it is important to utilize whatever the subject's model of the world will find acceptable. If the subject cannot relate to the context of the disassociation, their subconscious will void or limit the effectiveness of this and any other proposed intervention.

Anesthesia

The goal of this intervention is to remove or make numb the pain in a given area of the body. This is ideal for working with burn victims and dental patients. With these types of subjects you can easily consider removing one hundred percent of their pain. For other patients it usually is not recommended to remove all their pain for a prolonged period of time, as there will be a strong possibility for them to re-injure themselves. Also another negative possibility is that with all the pain removed and a certain area of the body numbed, the individual may feel handicapped.

To numb a certain area of the body you simply take the subject down into trance to the state of somnambulism and explain to them that a certain area of the body is becoming numb and without feelings. The other easy option is take your subject down to the Coma state where they automatically lose all sensations of feeling. Another possibility is to take your subject into trance to a state of somnambulism and have them make their hand numb, and then tell them to rub their hand on the body part that needs to lose the sensation of feeling. This way the numbness can be easily transferred from one body part to another. This procedure is fairly popular with dental work.

Analgesia

Analgesia is quite similar to anesthesia, but the subject's pain is reduced and the tactile sensation and pressure are still there. I would recommend approaching the subject in trance using terms of analogies to remove pain. A good example would be using: "Melting slowly away like a small ice cube in the sun". Thus, the pain will gradually start slipping away from the subject. In trance you may need to repeat yourself three times slowly so that the subconscious mind draws the suggestion from the analogy and puts it to work. This has proven to be quite effective with headaches of all types.

Symptom Substitution

The intent of this intervention is to replace the original uncomfortable feelings with a better feeling. This works in direct opposition to the current uncomfortable feeling. In trance you would describe the pain as warm instead of cold, or comfortably cool instead of hot. It is important to reinforce this idea in trance at least three times and establish a time line for this to occur, i.e.: two days, one week, ten days, etc. Even with symptom substitution you must maintain your concern for empowering your subject to the point of where they may re-injure themselves. The natural process of pain is the body's warning system for the individual and must be dealt with very carefully.

Fractional Approach to Pain Management

This intervention is based on the idea of turning down the individual's pain by using a percentage. Bearing in mind that we are not going for 100% pain removal, we will aim for 80% pain removal. In trance take the subject down to somnambulism and start at 10% pain reduction. Then slowly work forward in 10% increments to about 90% pain removal and tell your subject that we should settle for 80% of pain removal. In this manner we have reduced the pain without total pain removal, leaving the individual with their body's warning system intact in the event they start to do something to re-injure them selves once they leave your presence.

Auto Hypnosis

This is probably the best approach to pain management if the subject can deal with learning self-hypnosis at the time. By using self-hypnosis we can put the individual in charge of managing their own pain. This approach constitutes teaching your subject self-hypnosis and working with them briefly to develop their suggestions using the rules of auto -suggestion outlined in the chapter on self-hypnosis.

If your hypnotic subject has the presence of mind to learn self-hypnosis in their painful condition, the pay value for them will be well worth the effort. This intervention like the others does need follow up and sometimes reinforced with trance work.

I would like to also offer a non-hypnotic intervention for headaches that works very well. This intervention has the person visually disassociating from the headache. First ask the individual to assign a color to their headache. Once that is done ask the subject to make that color a shade lighter. Continue going lighter, switching to other lighter colors as you go. Keep this intervention up until you have the subject change colors at least five times. It is best to work with pastels whenever possible, and stay away from a stark white. This is a very simple but highly effective procedure for the treatment of headaches without even the benefit of trance work.

Another common problem associated with pain management is the treatment of children for blood draws and injections. Many a parent and nurses dread needles and children. This is a simplified technique you can use with young children; a simple rhyme will help young children to concentrate. They capture a child's imagination, helping him to learn just as some instructive nursery rhymes teach new concepts to smaller children. Here is a sample of a simple rhyme to have children memorize:

"Fairy, fairy, prove to me just how easy this can be. I'll close my eyes and see you smile and watch you dancing all the while. While you're dancing in the light everything will be all right. Fair fairy, prove to me just how easy this can be".

Probably the best way to use this rhyme is to have the child close his eyes and see a fairy dancing in his mind's eye. Then say to the child, "So long as you see that fairy dancing nothing will bother or disturb you." This technique is excellent for any treatment of short duration. It works wonderfully for injections and blood draws. Try it with a child once and you will be delighted with the results.

This other intervention known as the "Magic Spot" is very effective with adults as well as children. This example is also known as waking hypnosis based on the thought that the essence of hypnosis is the suggestion. The following is a sample script for applying the "Magic Spot."

I want you to open your eyes wide, now close your eyes and pretend that you can't open your eyes and keep on pretending you can't open your eyes, so much that when you try to open your eyes they just won't open. Now let me see you try to open them while you're pretending, that's right, now stay like that and keep on pretending you can't open your eyes, and the most amazing thing is going to happen. You're going to have a Magic Spot on your arm. Once this Magic Spot is put on you, never again will you have to feel an injection. You'll know that the doctor is working there, but nothing will disturb, nothing will bother you. You'll never have any discomfort from an injection, either before, during or afterwards…(Now paint the Magic Spot with an alcohol wipe and give the injection). Now you have had your injection and you know you didn't feel a thing. From now on you will always be able to have injections this easily. After a while that Magic Spot will no longer be visible to you or anyone else, except for one important thing, you will know exactly where it is so that any time you must receive an injection, you will be able to point out the exact area to the doctor. If you want, you will be able to watch him giving you the injection and it won't bother you a bit, all right now, open your eyes.

From that time on, the individual will always be able to access their own "Magic Spot". The proof of the effectiveness is in doing it once; after that you will surely be sold on this simple intervention. Pain, irregardless if we feel it is real or false, still remains real to that individual's model of the world.

Analogies and Metaphors
as Curative Factors

Metaphors have been used since before the time of Christ. By the very nature of metaphors it is impossible to find an approximate starting date of when metaphors were first used in a curative fashion. The first written metaphors used in a curative manner are found in the Christian Bible. A metaphor by another name is a parable. The bible is rich with these curative metaphors as teaching stories as they were supposedly told by Christ.

The best working definition of a metaphor is: An object, activity, or idea treated as a metaphor or a figure of speech in which a word or phrase literally denoting one kind of object or idea is used in place of another to suggest a likeness between them.

The uses of metaphors are many, but are generally understood to impact information and help build insight. The uses generally assist the individual with an entirely different and non-threatening look at their situation. Metaphorically explained, "It provides the individual an opportunity to get out of the trees and take a look at the forest they have been wandering around in". The fundamental characters and events which occur in the story are equivalent with those individuals and events which characterize the individual's situation. The term used for this is "Isomorphism" making a story

"Isomorphic" in comparison to the individual's own life situation." Thus, each person's own real significant involved in the individual's problem is represented in the metaphor's cast of characters. To include the parameters of the situation and processes are also represented. These representations are not equal to the parameters of the problem, but are equivalent in the sense of maintaining the same relationships among the parameters in the metaphor as those found in the actual situation.

Isomorphism is the metaphorical preservation of the relationships occurring in the actual problem situation. When constructing an effective metaphor it is not sufficient to only include in the story one character for each actual participant, or a one story line incident for each actual event. The relationships and sequence of the actual situation must be preserved in the story in order for the client to accept it as asignificant representation of their problem. What is significant about a metaphor is that it isomorphically represents the relationships and processes that is found in the problem. Any context is suitable for a metaphor provided the isomorphism is satisfied.

In selecting characters for a metaphor it is of no consequence what they are, really all that matters is how they are related. In the following example the characters share many of the same logical relationships as do the actual family members:

Actual		Metaphor
Father	(Becomes)	General
Mother	(Becomes)	Major
Son	(Becomes)	2d Lt
Father rarely home	(Becomes)	General often shut-up alone in office.
Son gets into trouble	(Becomes)	2d Lt makes bad decision.

Mother covers for son	(Becomes)	Major corrects the decision
Father finds out	(Becomes)	General finds out
No resolution	(Becomes)	Find resolution

Since the isomorphic meaning in this example is concerned only with relationships and not with context, there are no limitations on the nature of the context or the identity of the characters we use. Other characters that could be used in this metaphor could have been a pair of ships and a sailboat, or two trees and a sapling, or a stallion, a mare, and a colt.

It is important to allow the individual to draw their own interpretation of the metaphor. When offering someone a metaphor, it is often very tempting to also offer an interpretation of the metaphor. The metaphor is best served if the individual is allowed to reach their own conclusions. The subconscious will keep what is important in the metaphor and discard. the irrelevant information. We tend to construct our world through our perceptions and categories of thought that make up our own unique model of the world. This why we need to construct the metaphors taking into account the individual's model of the world. A metaphor about sailing a ship around the horn for a potato farmer in Idaho may not be a good idea, while a metaphor about growing tomatoes might be ideal.

There are two basic forms of metaphors commonly used. One is a metaphor constructed for an individual and their situation. The second form of metaphors is generic in nature, applicable to society at large. The aforementioned information has been directed to "tailoring" a metaphor for an individual. Now I would like to offer a generic form of a metaphor. The context of these metaphors are very generalized and will normally apply to most people. The following metaphor is a short offering of what a generic metaphor might appear as:

Bandits Metaphor

I want to share this story with you about two cowboys who became bandits; they decided to become bank robbers. They thought that would provide them a great deal of money. They had a great deal of trouble deciding which town in south Texas they would rob their first bank in. After weeks of discussing which town, they gave up and decided to rob the bank of the town they were already in. The cowboys entered the bank the following month and proceeded to rob it. As they ran from the bank and jumped on their horses the alarm was sounded. As they rode out of town there was already a posse being formed to chase them. They rode hard and fast toward Old Mexico to gain safety. When they reached the Rio Grande River they found that the river was high and flooding its banks, so they discovered they must change directions. To the east were mountains, but they couldn't decide, they were fearful they would freeze to death in the mountains. To the west was a desert, but they couldn't decide, they were fearful they would die of thirst in the desert. To the north the posse was coming after them, they couldn't go that way for fear the posse would shoot or hang them. What were they to do; they just couldn't seem to decide. So they sat down and died.

The intent of this generic metaphor was for use with individuals who have problems with procrastination. The intent of the metaphor is clear, while at the same time it is not isomorphic to any one person. Many of our fairy tales and folklore in our society are also metaphoric in nature. Tailored metaphors or generic metaphors, they both give us an opportunity to look at our problems from a different view without having to take direct ownership of the problem. Then our subconscious can take the curative information that it finds relevant and apply it to the individual and their situation.

Hypnotherapy, the use of hypnosis in therapy has drawn clear lines between the use of metaphors. There are metaphors specifically for children and metaphors for adults. The generally accepted age break point is thirteen years old. It is my contention that there are three age categories. The first category is from birth through age twelve. The second category is from age thirteen through age nineteen, and thirdly from age twenty and up. By the standards used by most clinical hypnotherapists who use metaphors the adolescents are overlooked and wrongfully placed with adults.

The main justification I offer for a separate category for adolescents is that there is a separate sub-culture that they exist in. The teenage subculture has it's own language, complete with their separate code of conduct. Thereby, adult language is far less impactful in meaning than their specific definition of words. The best example I can offer is the word "bad". To adults this is a negative word, but for most teenagers it usually means very good. By continuing to overlook the obvious mistake with applying adult metaphors to teenagers leaves them short-changed in our community of hypnotherapists and society in general.

To successfully construct curative metaphors for teenagers, the therapist must take into account the rather unique reality that our adolescents survive in and the separateness that exists from the child and the adult world. To establish a correct isomorphism the therapist must "tailor" the metaphor in the language that exists within our teenage culture. It has been my experience while consulting with other professionals to find a great number will avoid working with adolescents due to the teenager's fast paced, ever changing world. They often complain that it seems nearly impossible to keep abreast of all the linguistic adolescent changes as they occur.

There are two reasonable methods a therapist could use to obtain this adolescent linguistic information. The method I most highly recommend is that the therapist spend two sessions with the teenager before attempting to use a metaphor in a hypnotic trance. This would allow the therapist the time to pick likely words and phrases that would be used by that individual teenager. The least desirable method would be to use a generic metaphor in trance. These generic metaphors do have their place in therapy, especially if the therapist is time driven by the needs of the individual. Any positive metaphor offered to an individual has a curative factor to one degree or another. The simplest two generic metaphoric tips that I often teach are; (1) Reverse the subject's first name. By pronouncing the subject's name backwards, some degree of isomorphism is achieved. In a state of somnambulistic trance, the subject's subconscious can identify the isomorphism. (2) Record the metaphor on a cassette tape for the subject to listen to on a daily basis in-between hypnotic sessions. Much like homework, this allows the subject to more fully participate in their treatment. The more actively a subject is involved first hand in their treatment, the likelihood of success increases proportionate. At this time I would offer the following generic metaphor as an example to illustrate the point of making a metaphor isomorphic with the use of the patient's name pronounced backwards. This patient's name was Sandy, and suffered with low self-esteem. At this time I would like to offer the following generic metaphor as an example to illustrate the point of making a metaphor isomorphic with the use of the patient's name pronounced backwards. This patient's name was Sandy, and suffered with low self-esteem.

Play land

Ydnas, there is a nice story that I want to share with you. It's about Alice in Wonderland. I was wondering what Alice must have felt as she met all those unusual creatures and heard all those strange words, but kept going on her way not knowing what to expect that day, not knowing what is next or where to go might seem to be strange at first. After a while it becomes an adventure that delights the child and interests the mind. Because you never do know what's next, what will be. You can know that it is okay not to know what the future holds in store. Things change over time and things change in the mind, as your unconscious mind changes your mind about how things feel and are, like Alice when she saw that bottle that said, "drink me" on the label, when she did she got larger, then smaller than she had ever been before, or at least it seemed that way to her. It may be interesting to notice that when people relax, things begin to change; one arm may seem higher than the other. A leg may seem heavier then before, and even the entire body becomes more difficult to find. It may seem to float at times, or to get smaller and smaller as the chair feels bigger and bigger. The feet seem to change in some way while the hands do it differently. In a while you begin to wonder how you'll ever put it all back together just the way it belongs. How does it belong, really? What is the way it should be, because taste changes over time. So what we prefer today is not what we'll want tomorrow. What seems to be exactly right now, may be what is left over later on. Everywhere you look things are moving, rearranging. So it is hard to know what is the way things ought to be. In summer, trees are in full bloom, though their flowers are no longer there, in the autumn, greens change, become reds, oranges, browns and yellows. In winter they're all gone and begin next spring. Only now a new limb grows here and the old one dies there. How should that tree be, taller or shorter, more leaves or fewer, greener or rounder perhaps. Though there are those who might say that the tree is just the way it is. The way it is, is all it needs to be. The way they see a newborn child, each tiny finger exactly perfect. Each tiny ear perfectly exact. Though no two look exactly the same, Ydnas, like Alice in Wonderland. Where everything seems different, and she discovered how it felt to love being just what she was.

The telling of a metaphor in trance must be slow and deliberate in nature. The tempo of the metaphor should be slow enough to match the patient's breathing rate. This allows the subconscious mind enough time to assimilate the information as it is presented. Also during trance the metaphor should be spoken without verbal punctuation, a continual flow of words with appropriate pauses to match the breathing pattern. Then the subconscious mind will take what it feel's is important and discard the rest of the information.

The usefulness of metaphors in hypnotherapy has been debated over the years without complete agreement. However, I do strongly advocate the use of metaphors.

The following is a metaphoric example of its use applied to the problem of smoking.

Smoking Abstinence Metaphor

Take the client down to a medium state of trance and read the script while pacing their breathing pattern.

Now many people have come to me and asked for help with some particular difficulty and they say to me, "I have no motivation, I have no discipline". And I say to them, "The unmotivated person doesn't call for an appointment. The undisciplined person doesn't show up on time". The unmotivated person does not distinguish the place they wish to be, from the place where they are now. The undisciplined person stays home. Now you have all the motivation you need, you have all the discipline you need, though there is one thing you still need which you don't have yet, and that's self-confidence, the self-confidence it takes to set out on a journey completely prepared for the trip, knowing you've read the map, you've charted the course, reservations taken care of, believing you can, will, reach your destination quickly, easily, effortlessly. The self-confidence it takes to recognize all the signs of success. Just as now, you recognize those comfortable hypnotic sensations in the hands, arms, legs. Those physical signs that allow you to know you've traveled from one state to another state in a calm, confident way, and you can offer yourself large portions of self-confidence, large portions of self-esteem, you can breathe in self-confidence and breathe out self doubt as you continue to enjoy the journey towards your goal. Throughout the years that I have worked with people I have had many clients come here with a particularity interesting problem. They have become obsessed with the idea of making love with someone they are attracted to, and when they have raised the subject with the object of their desire they've been told, in no uncertain terms, that a physical relationship was an impossibility, and the reasons given for the impossibility have been many. It is to dangerous or risky, unhealthy or even unethical, and yet, faced with all these obstacles, these clients become more and more obsessed, convinced that their happiness depends on the consummation of their desires, to the neglect of all other aspects of their lives. Which reminds me of the man who had just bought a brand new house, an expensive house, in the nicest part of town, he had admired that house for many, many years, maybe since he was a teenager, maybe from his twenties, he couldn't remember exactly, but he did know he'd been wanting to buy that house for a long, long time, and now here it was ... all his, he lavished care and attention on it, decorated it in tasteful colors of (insert color of client's clothing). He papered and painted and hardly paid any attention at all to that growing headache at first, in fact it was several years before he noticed that his head seemed to have a continual dull ache, and his muscles were aching as well, he felt tired a lot, too, so he visited a doctor who gave him a prescription, but he just never felt much better and everything failed to stop that headache, or the irritation and the insidious feeling that his health was fading, away, but at least he had his house and it is easy to understand how he might feel if you've ever gone from house to house, real estate open houses perhaps, or just going to someone else's home, seeing how the other half lives can be an educational experience, but I can understand my client's obsession with something that's not about to happen, from the day I saw my dream house, of course the price was very beyond what I could possibly afford, and yet I couldn't get it out of my mind, I imagined myself in the living room, in the den, and was certain I must have it to be happy. Now everybody knows that nobody likes to be told what to do, and if I could tell you what to do you wouldn't have to be here today. You'd call me on the phone, it you'd say, "I'd like to quit smoking", and I would say, "That's a wonderful idea, quit smoking now". But everybody knows nobody likes to be told what to do, so I won't say to you, you already know all the reasons for ending this smoking problem, I wouldn't have to say to you that smoking is dangerous and unhealthy. I wouldn't have to tell you that you will receive no pleasure from smoking, I never need to say that cigarettes are a poor substitute for (insert client's rational for smoking), but one thing I will say to you is; "Not smoking is not a task you wouldn't find easy" when you leave here today you'll no longer be somebody who smokes, You know you have the desire to smoke, and no one can talk you out of it, but you have a very, very huge, a very large amount of NO DESIRE, and you can get to know this place of no desire as it expands and grows larger and larger, and the feeling of no desire can reach deeper and deeper, the time of no desire continues to lengthen, and no way is easier than this, and I read once. When I was a child, I thought like a child, I acted like a child. Now that I am grown I put away the things of childhood, what does that really mean? I'm not sure, but it certainly meant a lot to clients who were obsessed with a sexual desire that could never be fulfilled. Perhaps it was the thought of putting old ways behind them that finally allowed them to be free, or perhaps they simply grew up and took responsibility for their feelings and their behavior. Disappointment is something we all face from time to time, and you can imagine how disappointed that man was to learn there was insecticide in the floor and walls of that house. He went on his dream vacation, and was amazed to discover his headaches and sickness disappeared in just a few days time. When he got home he contacted an expert in the field. The expert gently broke the news, his entire house was slowly being poisoned, and so was he. It only took him one day to pack his things. He knew for certain his health was worth more than any house ... no matter how long he'd wanted it, and I guess I finally came to terms with the fact that I couldn't buy a $300,000 home, no matter what I did. It was a nice dream, but the price was to high to pay, especially since there was no Jacuzzi, letting go, not needing to now how the unconscious mind knows what to do for you, thinking with an awareness of things thought, without needing to know those things which will get done automatically, you know what to do, now I'd prefer you stop smoking immediately, but it's entirely up to you to discover, today, the best time and way for you. Some clients wait an hour, some wait until after dinner, some stop entirely right before bed. Now, I'd prefer you stop immediately, but it's completely up to you to choose the time, a time today, when you free yourself from smoking forever.

Self Hypnosis

Self-hypnosis is a familiar term for most people in our society. The correct term for self-hypnosis is Autohypnosis. The correct terminology for when you hypnotize someone is hetrohypnosis. The practice of self- hypnosis is as old as hetro-hypnosis. Indian tribes, religious people in savage tribes, and faith healers of days long gone, appeared to assume some supernatural power and were able to anaesthetize different parts of their bodies spontaneously. This enabled them to walk barefooted on a bed of hot coals, or sleep on a bed of nails, etc. Self-hypnosis entered the scientific community a hundred years after hetro-hypnosis.

The pioneer of self-hypnosis was a young French pharmacist called Emil Cotie. Cotie's famous autosuggestion formula is "Every day, in every way, I am getting better and better." The theories and rules for self-hypnosis are similar to those explained for hetro-hypnosis. There is, however, no direct research to show whether these two phenomena are alike, that is whether the same abilities, ego functioning and personality traits are involved in both.

In most textbooks there is three fundamental attitudes which should accompany the induction of self-hypnosis. These are:

1. "I want to remember what happened in hypnosis as a conscious state of mind.

2. "I expect this to happen." Generate a belief in your ability to achieve what millions before you have attained. Remember hypnosis is just another one of nature's normal states.

3. "I will watch it happen." Once you begin to respond properly do not allow yourself to hinder the carrying out of suggestions by letting your critical factor re-enter and change your mood.

There are a number of mechanical aids that can help a person to induce self-hypnosis and deepen the hypnotic trance. These mechanical aids include hypnotic crystal balls, metronomes, hypnodisck and hypnospirals. Some of these aids may suit the individual needs of a person, some may not. If a person wants to take advantage of one of these mechanical aids, he has to choose it on the basis of psychological. preference. One of the easiest ways to induce self-hypnosis is to record your own hypnotic induction or have someone else with a good speaking voice read it to you. The patter should be property worded, soothing, and monotone. Deepening procedures can also be carried out by listening to a tape made for that purpose.

To be most effective, these tapes should be recorded in the second person, instead of saying, "My body is getting numb and heavy." This is because in the induction process your conscious mind is the hypnotist and your subconscious mind is the subject.

Irregardless of the approach one takes to hypnosis it is important to recognize that the suggestion is actually the sole agent of hypnosis and the exclusive means of behavior modification. When a person suggests thoughts and ideas to themselves, they have already reasoned them out and have faith in them. Even in hetrohypnosis the suggestions of the hypnotist do not take effect without the unconscious agreement of the subject.

We know that whenever there is a clash between the conscious and subconscious minds, the subconscious mind always wins.

Therefore, for a suggestion to be carried out by the conscious mind, acceptance by the unconscious mind is necessary. It follows that autosuggestion is usually much more meaningful than suggestions administered by some one else. Moreover, when a person lives suggestions to himself he will, in fact, participate directly and more actively in his behavior modification goal's than when induced to do so by another person.

The most effective method of autosuggestion is probably a combination of pre-hypnotic and pictorial suggestions. The person will word his suggestion after meeting the preparatory conditions, and before self-hypnosis. When he has achieved self-hypnosis, his visual image will reflect his suggestion. In conveying suggestions to the unconscious mind, picture images seem to be more effective than words. This is because the unconscious mind understands pictures better than words. There is much truth in the saying, "A picture is worth a thousand words".

There are five rules of autosuggestion that are generally accepted in professional circles. These are:

1. Suggestions should be condensed, revised, and perfected on a piece of paper and read several times prior to the induction of self-hypnosis.
2. Auto-suggestions should be direct, permissive, and positive. Negative words and phrases such as "not", "can't", "won't", should be avoided. Example (for a headache) upon awaking, " My headache will be gone". It would be better to suggest, "my head is feeling clear and better, I am becoming more and more comfortable and tranquil in every way". Another advantage of applying this procedure is that the unconscious mind will be given sufficient time to assimilate the idea.
3. The suggestion should be combined with a motive that enhances the effectiveness of the suggestion. This may be done through visual imagery. When a person gives himself a

suggestion to overcome tension at the time of a job interview he may envision getting a good prestigious job instead of saying to himself not to be nervous and tense during the interview.

4. Suggestions should be given singularly. The unconscious mind cannot deal with more than one idea at a time. Additionally, the suggestion should be repeated and reinforced in successive hypnotic sessions until the desired goal is achieved.
5. Auto-suggestions should be positively and logically worded and capable of being fulfilled.

Hypnosis, whether hetro-hypnosis or self-hypnosis, is simply an end in itself, but a means that can be used for self-improvement and therapeutic purposes.

Deepening Procedures for Self Hypnosis

Although light to deep trance has the same effect for the unconscious mind to assimilate the autosuggestion, to deepen autohypnosis, a number of techniques can be applied, some of which are common to hetro-hypnosis.

Visual Imagery Technique

This is one of the best techniques for deepening self-hypnosis. You imagine yourself in any situation that gives you peace and serenity.

For instance, you may see yourself lying down comfortably in your bed enjoying a sound sleep and pleasant dreams; or you may be lying in a hammock, or lying on a beach and watching the ocean waves, or any similar relaxing imagery. As you imagine yourself in such desirable conditions, concentrate on drifting deeper and deeper into relaxation.

Escalator Technique

You may imagine yourself riding down an escalator. Then you start counting slowly to yourself from twenty to zero. You should think to yourself that the further the escalator goes down, the deeper you go into hypnosis. Also, between each number you may imagine yourself drifting deeper into relaxation.

Counting Method

You may count from 100 forwards or backwards, and by one's, two's, three's four's, etc. With every count you should imagine yourself drifting deeper and deeper into relaxation. Deepening self-hypnosis requires the same kind of practice or conditioning as the induction of hypnosis. Therefore, with every count, you should coordinate your bodily functioning with your thoughts. For instance, you should designate a particular number by which time you feel your mind is separated from your body.

Hand Levitation Method

You may suggest hand levitation to yourself and imagine that when your fingers touch your face, your arm will immediately become heavy and fall to your thigh.

Post-Hypnotic Suggestion

As with hetro-hypnosis, each time you hypnotize yourself you can give the suggestion that the next time you attempt self-hypnosis you will go more quickly and more deeply into the hypnotic state.

These are the more standard approaches to deepening Self-Hypnosis. If you are using a cassette tape make sure you incorporate the deepening techniques throughout your induction.

Deep Muscle
Relaxation Training

This is the first of a three-phase program to prepare you for Self-Hypnosis. The end result of this session is for you to have a heightened sense of awareness of what it feels like for your body to be relaxed. This technique alone will not teach you every thing you need to know. It is imperative that you practice all three phases of this program. The number of seconds to pause is denoted by the number in parentisis (0).

(Script)

We will begin with you becoming comfortable. (10) You can either be sitting down in a chair or lying down. If you use a chair, try to make it one with arms, if lying down, do not use a pillow. If your clothing is too tight and uncomfortable, loosen it slightly now (4). Settle back now as comfortable as you can (4). Focus your attention on my voice (3). As other thoughts drift into your mind, let them drift away and continue to focus on my voice only (4). (Spend four minutes talking the client through a deep breathing exercise.). As you relax, clench your right fist, now clench your fist tighter and tighter, and study the tension in your right fist and forearm. You can feel the tension become uncomfortable in your right fist and forearm. You can feel the tension become uncomfortable in your right fist as you keep it tightly clenched (3). Now relax (4). Let the fingers of your right hand become loose (5). Observe the contrast in the feelings of your right hand (5). Let yourself go and try to become more relaxed all over (5.). Once more again, clench your right fist really tight (3). Hold it tight (13). Now notice the tension again, it feels very tight and uncomfortable (2). Now let go (2). Relax more; notice the difference once more (10). Now we will repeat that with your left hand and forearm (,2). Clench your left fist while the rest of your body relaxes (3.). Clench your fist tight and feel the tension (3.).

Now relax (5). Again, enjoy the contrast in feelings (4,). Let your mind focus on that feeling of relaxation. Repeat that once more, clench your left fist (.3). Make your fist very tight and tense (3). Now relax and feel the difference (4). Slowly straighten out your fingers (10). Clench both fists now (3). Tight, and tighter (2).

Both fists tense, forearms tense, study the sensation (2). Relax now (2). Let the feelings of relaxation flow into both hands (2). Straighten out your fingers and feel the relaxation (3). Continue relaxing your hands and forearms more and more (13). Now bend both your elbows and tense your biceps by pulling your hands towards your shoulders (3). Tense them tighter and study the feelings of tension (5). Now straighten out your arms (4). Let them relax, and now feel the difference again (3). Let the relaxation develop (8). Once more, tense your biceps (14.). Hold that tension and observe it carefully (4). Straighten your arms and allow the feelings of relaxation to flow into yours arms (4.). Relax to the best of your ability (8,). Now straighten your arms so that you feel the most tension in the triceps muscle along the back of your arms (3). Now relax (5.). Move your arms back into a comfortable position (5). Let the relaxation flow on its own accord (8). Your arms should feel comfortably heavy as you allow the relaxation to flow (5). Once more, straighten your arms so that you feel the tension in your triceps (8). Let your arms relax again and focus on the comfortable feelings of relaxation in your arms (6). Now let's focus on pure relaxation in the arms without any tension. Move your arms into a comfortable position and let them relax (8). Let the relaxation flow into your arms, (3). Focus on that nice warm feeling in your arms (10). Even when your arms seem fully relaxed, try to let your arms achieve a deeper level of relaxation (12). Now we will move upwards to the head and shoulders (2). We will start by letting all your muscles go loose and heavy. Just settle back quietly and comfortably. Wrinkle up your forehead now (3). Wrinkle it tighter (5). Now stop wrinkling your forehead (4). Relax and allow it to smooth out (3). Picture your entire forehead and scalp becoming smoother as the relaxation increases (10). Now frown and crease your brows and study the tension (6). Let go of the tension once again,smooth out your forehead once more (10). Now close your eyes tighter and tighter (5). Feel the tension (3). Now relax your eyes (4). Keep your eyes closed gently, comfortably and notice the relaxation (10). Now clench your jaws (10). Relax your jaws now, let your lips part slightly (6). Appreciate the feeling of relaxation (12). Now press your tongue hard against the roof of your mouth (4). Look for the tension (4). All right, let your tongue return to a comfortable and relaxed position Now press your lips together (4). Tighter and tighter, relax your lips, note the contrast between tension and relaxation (8). Feel the relaxation all over your face (8).

Now to attend to your neck muscles, press your head back as far as it can go and feel the tension in your neck (31). Roll it to the right and feel the tension shift (3). Now roll it to the left (3). Straighten your head and bring it forward and Press your chin against your chest (4). Let your head return to a comfortable position, and study the relaxation Let the relaxation develop (10).

Now shrug your shoulders straight up. Hold the tension (4). Drop your shoulders slowly and feel the relaxation (4). Feel your neck and shoulders relaxing (8). Shrug your shoulders up and forward (4). Now back, feel the tension in your shoulders and in your upper back (4). Drop your shoulders slowly once more and relax (6). Let the relaxation spread deeply into your shoulders, right into your back muscles (6). Relax your neck and throat, and your jaw and other facial areas as the pure relaxation takes over and goes deeper (3). Deeper, even deeper (10). Allow yourself to focus on the warm, heavy comfortable feeling in your face and shoulders (12). If other thoughts drift into your mind, let them drift on by and continue to focus on my voice (8). We now shift our focus to the trunk of your body, start with relaxing your entire body to the best of your ability (8). Feel that comfortable heaviness that accompanies relaxation (8). Breathe easily and freely, in and out (15). Notice how the relaxation increases as you exhale (10). As you breathe out, feel that relaxation (4). Now breathe in and fill up your lungs, inhale deeply and hold your breath (4). Study the sensation (3). Now exhale, let the walls of your chest grow loose and push the air out automatically (3). Continue relaxing and breathe freely and gently (6). Feel the relaxation and enjoy it (8). With the rest of your body as relaxed as possible, fill your lungs again (8). That's fine, breath out, and again, breathe in deeply and hold it (8). Now breathe out and appreciate the relief (4). Just breathe normally (6). Continuing relaxing your chest and let the relaxation spread to your back (6). To your shoulders (6). To your neck (6). To your arms (6). Merely let go and enjoy the relaxation (12). Now let's pay attention to your abdominal muscles, pull your stomach in, pull the muscles right in and feel the tension this way.

Now relax again, let your stomach out . Continue to breathe normally and easily and feel the gentle massaging action all over your chest and stomach (12). Now pull your stomach in again and hold the tension (8). Release the tension (8). Once more pull in your stomach fully and feel the tension (8). Now relax your stomach fully (3). Let the tension dissolve as the relaxation grows deeper (6). Each time you breathe out notice the rhythmic relaxation both in your lungs and in your stomach (10). Notice how your chest and stomach relaxes more and more (8). Try and let go of all the muscle tension anywhere in your body (12). Now direct your attention to your lower back (3). Arch up your back, make your lower back hollow, and feel the tension along your spine (4). Now settle back comfortably again, relaxing the lower back (10). Arch your back up again and feel the tension as you do so. Try to keep the rest of your body relaxed as possible. Try to localize the tension throughout your lower back area (2). Relax once more (3). Relax your upper back (6). Spread the relaxation to your stomach (6). Now to your chest (6). Now to your shoulders (6). Now to your arms (6). Now to your facial area (6.). These parts are relaxing further and further, and now go even deeper (6). Let it flow as a warm, heavy, comfortable feeling (12). Let go of all tensions and just relax (8). Now flex your buttocks and thighs. Flex your thighs by pressing down your heels as hard as you can (6). Relax and note the difference (8). Straighten your knees and flex your thigh muscles again, hold the tension (6). Relax your hips and thighs (8). Allow the relaxation to proceed on its own (10). Press your feet and toes downwards, away from your face, so that calf muscles become tense, study that tension (6). Relax your feet and calves (8). This time, bend your feet away from your face so that you feel tension along your shins, (6) bring your toes back up, (2) relax again. (6) Keep relaxing for awhile (6),now let yourself relax further all over (6). Relax your feet (6). Relax your ankles now (6). Relax your calves now (6). Relax your shins now (6). Relax your knees now (6). Relax your thighs now (6). Relax your buttocks now (6). Relax your hips now (6). Feel the heaviness of your lower body as you relax still further. Let go now, more and more (4). Feel that relaxation all over. Let it proceed to your upper back (6). Keep relaxing more and more deeply (20). Make sure that no tension has crept into your throat (2). Relax your neck and your jaws and all your facial muscles (4). Keep relaxing your whole body like that for a while. Let yourself totally relax (12). Now you can become twice as relaxed by taking in a really deep breath and slowly exhaling (6). Close your eyes so that you become less aware of objects and movements around you, and prevent any surface tensions from developing (8). Breathe in deeply and feel yourself becoming heavier (5). Take a long deep breath and let it out very slowly (6). Feel how heavy and relaxed you have become (12). The relaxation is flowing through you in a warm and comfortable way (30). In a state of Perfect relaxation you should feel unwilling to move a single muscle in your body (3). Think about the effort that would be required to raise your right arm, as you think about raising your right arm, see if you can notice any tensions that might have crept into your right shoulder and your arm (6). Now you decide not to lift your arm, but to continue relaxing (12). Observe the relief and the disappearance of the tension (6). Just continue relaxing like that (12). When you wish to get up, count backward from five to one (6). You should then feel fine and refreshed, wide-awake and calm, slowly open your eyes and look about (4). Flex your fingers and toes slightly. Now in a slow and easy manner you can bring yourself to your feet (6).

It may be necessary for you to repeat this exercise several times to develop a strong sense of awareness of what your body feels like to be relaxed. The value of this exercise is for you to develop a heightened sense of awareness of the feelings of relaxation, and the feelings of tension.

Now you are ready to leave the Deep Muscle Relaxation phase and move on to the Muscle Relaxation phase of this training.

Muscle Relaxation Script

This is the second in a series of your relaxation training. Before moving into the second phase of this program lets take a minute to review the first phase. Hopefully, by now, you have repeated the first phase of relaxation and tension.

(Script)

During this phase I want you to mentally recall the feelings you experienced during the first session. Recall it slowly (10). Tighten and loosen your muscles if needed to re-awaken the feeling of relaxation (10). Settle back, and make yourself comfortable (15). Also recall the breathing exercises now that we are prepared (15). Lets move on (5). Begin with your feet, focus on your toes and feet, focus on that comfortable, warm, heavy feeling (10). If you find distracting thoughts drift into your mind, let them drift on by, don't try to force the thoughts out of yourself and your mind (3). Just let them drift on by (10). Focus now on the calves of your legs (10). Feel them grow heavier and heavier (10). Feel the tension drift away and that heavy comfortable feeling flow in (15). Now let that nice feeling of relaxation flow slowly upwards (15). You can feel it slowly working into your thighs (10). You're now feeling that nice warm heavy feeling spread throughout your thighs (10). Feel your thighs grow heavier and heavier (10). Feel the tension drift away and that heavy comfortable feeling flow freely. If you find distracting thoughts coming into your mind, let them drift on by and continue to focus on my voice Let that comfortable feeling move upwards into your hips and buttocks. Let that mental image become warm and heavy, very comfortable (15). The feeling is becoming very soothing and relaxing (15). The feeling becomes more and more comfortable as the tension drifts away (20).

Now feel that comfortable feeling move up into your stomach and lower back (10). Feel the tension start slowly drifting away (10). That comfortable feeling of relaxation is starting to flow in and feels so soothing and warm (10). The feeling of relaxation continues to grow and feel warmer and more comfortable (10). Don't hesitate to let your body relax and sink into a wonderful feeling of relaxation (15). It is now traveling upwards again, into your chest and shoulders (8). The tension is now flowing away (10). The tension still slowly drifting (10). The feeling of relaxation is now taking over in your chest and shoulders (15). Spreading so slowly, and. very relaxing (20). The feeling of relaxation becomes deeper and deeper (25). Now the feeling of relaxation is seeping down through your arms and into your hands (15).Now you feel your arms and hands grow warm and heavy (12). That heavy comfortable feeling is becoming more and more soothing (12). The tension has drifted out of arms and hands now, and the warm heavy feeling is flowing freely (10). Your arms and hands continue to grow warm and heavy (,10). Let the feeling of relaxation go deeper and deeper (20). Now let your mind slowly move to focus on your neck and scalp (15). Let the warm comfortable feeling spread up through your neck and into your scalp (10). The tension is slowly drifting away (12). Now the warm comfortable feeling is flowing and feeling better and better (12). Slowly you feel the warmth move you deeper and deeper into relaxation (15). The feeling of relaxation is now drifting down into your facial muscles

(10). The tension is drifting out now and that warm relaxed feeling is increasing (15). Now the warm heavy comfortable feeling is flowing with warmth and comfort (30). Now you are feeling that warm, heavy, comfortable feeling engulf your entire body (45). The feeling flows so freely into the warm wonderful feeling of relaxation (60). Now, very slowly count backwards from five to one (10). Now slowly move your toes (5). Now also move your fingers slightly (5). Open your eyes and slowly look about you (14). At this time you will start to feel. more alert and refreshed (6). You may feel free to get up now and move about. It is recommended that you practice this technique several times before moving on to Guided Imagery.

Guided Imagery

During this session we will focus on guided imagery as a means of relaxation. This is the third and final teaching phase in progressive relaxation techniques. We start this session with a reflective look back to the sessions of deep muscle techniques and muscle relaxation. Try to recall in your mind the feelings you experienced during these exercises. The (0) denote pauses in seconds.

Script

Assume a comfortable position before you begin to form the mental image of your body relaxing (6). Loosen any tight clothing and let the warm comfortable feeling of relaxation take over (12). If any distracting thoughts enter your mind, let them drift on by and continue to focus on the sound of my voice, and that warm, heavy and comfortable feeling that is starting to move through your body (15). If you have trouble recalling that feeling of relaxation at this time, stop briefly and perform phase one again of the awareness of relaxation in your body (15). Now mentally recreate that feeling of relaxation in your body (10). Let it begin with your toes (10). Slowly, that warm comfortable feeling starts moving upwards. Now moving into the calves of your legs. The warm heavy feeling is flowing stronger, but quite easily. The feeling now moves into your thighs (10).

Slowly and very warmly spreading (10). That warm comfortable feeling is now moving into your hips and buttocks (10).
Slowly and warmly the feeling of relaxation is spreading throughout your lower body (10). Feel- the warmth and comfort spread to
your stomach and lower back (10). Feel. those muscles gently let
go and the relaxation flow in (15). The warm feeling of comfort is
now spreading upwards through your chest and shoulders (10).
Progressing gently and slowly onwards up through your neck and
scalp (15). Take a minute now to dwell on the feeling you are
experiencing in your body. (60) Now that you have achieved a
state of relaxation , continue to focus on my voice as we create a
mental picture in your mind (10). Imagine yourself now, sitting
down and leaning against a huge tree in an open field (15). You
are sitting in lush, soft green area (15). You can feel a gentle warm
breeze (10). The breeze is soft and warm on your face (15). Just
like a soft warm caress (15). You feel very relaxed now, deeply
relaxed (10). A warm comfortable feeling holds your body and
mind in relaxation In your mind's eye you slowly turn and look
upwards, looking to the top of the tree filled with leaves. You see
that warm gentle breeze stirring the leaves on the tree, ever so
softly and gently (10). You casually notice that from the top of the
tree a leaf has broken away and is starting to fall (10). The warm
breeze is cradling the leaf (10). Rocking the leaf gently back and
forth (10). The leaf moves ever so slowly in the breeze (10). Feel
that warm gentle breeze again, gently touching your face (10).
Notice the free flowing relaxation going through your body (15).
You also notice that the leaf is still falling ever so slowly (10). It is
still being cradled and rocked, back and forth by the gentle warm
breeze you feel (15). The leaf is still slowly working its way down
in its descent to the ground (15). The leaf is moving so slowly and
unhurried (15). Still gently floating and moving so gracefully with
the breeze (15). Unhurried or bothered by time, the leaf continues

its slow and deliberate descent to the ground (15). Let your mind slowly turn inward to become re-aware of the wonderful state of relaxation your body is enjoying (20). That comfortable, warm heavy feeling continues to flow throughout your person (30). Now your mind slowly turns back to the leaf (5). It is sti11 making its graceful descent downwards (15). Still gently swaying in the breeze (10). Back and forth, so slowly and gently, as it moves to its downward destination (15). With slow graceful motion, the warm pleasant breeze you feel is sti11 carrying the leaf further downward (15). You. observe the leaf moving with gentle and tender grace (15). The leaf is being cradled by the warm breeze, you can also feel the warmness of your body relaxing, and the gentle warm breeze caressing you (20).

The leaf is moving slowly (10). Still making its unhurried descent to the ground below (20). The leaf is coming closer to the ground now (15). Still gently and slowly moving with an air of grace in its every movement (20). At times the leaf will appear almost to be suspended in the air by the gentle nurturing of the warm breeze (20). Now it appears to be in its final, but graceful descent (20). Slowly, with a gentle swaying motion, the leaf comes to rest beside you (10). The leaf, like you, has finally come to a complete state of rest. Gently let your mind explore your body in this state of relaxation (60). Now slowly count backwards from five to one (10). Slowly now, open your eyes and look about you (5).

Slowly move your toes and fingers, and you will find muscle tension returning.

To obtain the maximum amount of effectiveness from this session, it is recommended that you repeat this exercise several times over on your own. In time, the mental image of the failing leaf will become your key to unlocking your relaxation through your mind's association with this mental image. You may in the future decide to create your own personal image to better suit your personality. I would recommend you consult with an individual in the field of psychology for assistance and guidance. If you do not desire to seek out consultation, I would suggest you use a serene, calm scene for your mental image, such as a lake, snow covered mountain, etc.

Spiegel's Technique

This is another method of how to teach patients to hypnotize themselves and reinforce their therapeutic suggestions. Two psychiatrists who were brothers, Herbert and David Spiegel developed this technique.

You should advise your patients to do the following: Sit or lie down, and to yourself, you count to three. At one, you do one thing, at two, you do two things, at three, and you do three things. In all, you carry out six things. At one, look up towards your eyebrows; at two, while looking up, close your eyelids and take a deep breath, at three exhale, let your eyes relax, and let your body float.

As you feel yourself floating, you permit one hand or the other to feel like a buoyant balloon and let it float upwards. When it reaches this upright position, it becomes a signal for you to enter a state of meditation.

This floating sensation signals your mind to turn inward and pay attention to your own thoughts; like private meditation. Ballet dancers and athletes float all the time. That is why they concentrate and coordinate their movements so well. When they do not float they are tense and do not do as well.

Then the Spiegel's advise their patients that in the beginning they should do these exercises as often as ten different times a day, preferably every one or two hours. At first the exercise takes a minute, but as the patient becomes more experienced, he can do it in much less time.

Combination Method

Seat yourself in a comfortable chair with your feet flat on the floor, your legs extended, and your hands on your thighs or on the arms of the chair. Meet the preparatory rules for self-hypnosis. Fix your gaze on something above eye level.

Script

Begin counting slowly from 1 to 10. Say the number one, direct your attention on your eyes and tell yourself repeatedly, "My eyes are getting heavy, very heavy. I feel my eyes becoming so heavy at the count of 3 I will not be able to keep them open, they will close automatically". Count to two and think of the symbol "55". Roll your eyes up into the back of your head, then count to three and tell yourself, "My eyelids are so heavy now that I cannot open them. It is just as if they were glued together...I will now go deeper into self-relaxation. I am able to open my eyes whenever I choose, but I will keep them closed for the remainder of the induction".

Next, count to 4, think of the symbol "55", and give yourself the following suggestions; "My toes, feet, calves, and legs are getting very heavy. I feel a tingling sensation all over my legs. It feels very nice. Both my legs, from my toes up to the pelvic area feel stuck to the floor. I now go even deeper into self-relaxation. I am able to move my legs whenever I choose, and I now will go even deeper into self relaxation". Now, count to 5, think of the "55" and say to yourself, "I feel my abdominal muscles becoming numb and heavy. Even the pit of my stomach is becoming wooden-like and relaxed".

Count to 6, think of the image "55", and continue telling yourself, "Now I can feel the muscles in my chest becoming relaxed, I am breathing more regularly and more easily" (then thinking now and then of the symbol "55"), continue counting and with the count of 7, tell yourself), "Now I feel a numb, wooden-like sensation in my fingers, wrists, hands, arms and forearms. My arms feel just as though I have been sleeping on them. Eight, the muscles of my neck and my entire body, from my neck down, are relaxed. Nine, I feel my facial muscles becoming loose. My head is also very heavy and at the same time very relaxed and refreshed. My whole body feels loose and limp, from the top of my head right down to my toes. With every breath I take, I can feel myself drifting into a deeper and deeper state of relaxation". Then you have to visualize a very relaxed scene like the one described in the Subjective Technique. It can be some pleasant scene you imagine in the future. It can be a peaceful, mountainous scene, a blue sky with one or two billowy clouds moving slowly. On a lake with a sailboat floating gently, or any scene that makes you feel good, drowsy, and relaxed.

The "key word" and suggestions should be given at the appropriate time. The more practice you put into this procedure will be directly reflected in the outcome you achieve. This would be an excellent script to record on a cassette for your personal use.

Subjective Method

(Self-Hypnosis Technique)

Sit in a comfortable chair or lie down on a couch or bed. Fix your eyes on a spot on the wall above eye level or on the ceiling. Try to meet all the preparatory requirements for self-hypnosis. Then focus your attention on your eyelids. During the procedure think of the symbol "55". Now, first imagine that your eyelids are becoming very heavy. Try to feel this heaviness. Again and again tell yourself mentally; "My eyes are getting very heavy. I feel my eyes getting very heavy, and the heavier they become, the more comfortable and relaxed I feel. It seems that it is impossible for me to keep my eyelids open. It really feels so good to close my eyes. I am going count to three. When I complete the count, it will be absolutely impossible for me to keep my eyes open. One, my eyes are narrowing to a slit, they are about to close. Two, my eyelids are going to drop involuntarily. Three…they are closing, they are closing, they are closing". (Now tell yourself) "My eyelids are now locked together, they are stuck fast, so tightly that I can not open them. Now, do not try any longer, I can open my eyes whenever I choose, but will keep them closed for the remainder of the induction". Now think of a peaceful scene, imagine you are walking around a swimming pool in the middle of a beautiful garden.

It is mid spring, the weather is very pleasant. It is 3 o'clock in the afternoon, you keep walking alongside the pool. All around the pool are red, white and yellow roses. Alongside the pool are jasmine trees. A mild breeze blows from the flowers, bringing the sweet smell of roses and jasmine. As you continue walking, the sweet jasmine scent stays with you. Suddenly, a few yards from the pool, you see a hammock stretched between two shady trees. You decide to lie down in that hammock in the midst of the beautiful garden and enjoy a deep relaxation. So, you approach the hammock, you lie down in it, and find it very comfortable and relaxing. You feel so relaxed and comfortable that ten minutes of actual time pass like one minute. As you enjoy your relaxed state, a pretty bird lands on the branch of a tree in front of you. You keep looking at it. After a few seconds the bird leaves its perch and starts to fly toward you. It is getting closer and closer to you. You wish to follow the movements of the bird, but the beauty of the scene causes you to close your eyes and go into a very deep sleep.

Escalator Technique

(Self-Hypnosis Technique)

The technique used in this script is excellent for being able to go deep into Self-Hypnosis. This would also be a good script to put on a cassette tape for your use. Practice is the key to your success with any of these Self-Hypnotic techniques listed in this book.

Take a comfortable position in your chair. Close your eyes and breathe deeply two or three times. Now that you are comfortable, you will listen closely to my voice and follow all the suggestions given. Your eyes are now closed, take another deep breath, hold it a few seconds, and let it out. Mentally say to yourself, relax deeply, relax deeply. The more you can relax and the more you concentrate, the deeper you will go into hypnosis. Let all your muscles go as loose and limp as possible. To do this, start with your right leg, tighten the muscles first, make the leg rigid, then let it relax from your toe right up to your hip. Then tighten the muscles of the left leg, let that leg relax from the toes up to the hip. Let the stomach. and abdominal area relax, then your chest and breathing muscles. The muscles of your back can loosen, your shoulders and neck muscles relaxing. Often we have tension in these areas. Let all these muscles relax. Now your arms right down to your finger tips. Even your facial muscles will relax; relaxation is so pleasant and comfortable. Let go completely and enjoy the relaxation. All tension seems to drain away and you soon find a listlessness creeping over you, with a sense of comfort and well being. As you relax more and more, you will slip deeper and deeper into hypnosis. Your arms and legs may develop a feeling of heaviness, or instead you find your whole body feeling very light, as though you are floating on a soft cloud. Allow yourself to experience any such sensation you are having for a minute. Just let yourself go and feel the sensation of floating, or heaviness, or any other sensation you are experiencing (ten second pause). Now listen to me and imagine that you are standing at the top of an escalator such as those found in stores. See the steps moving down in front of you, and you see the railings. I am going to count from ten to zero, as I start to count, imagine that you are stepping on the escalator, standing there with your hands on the railing while the steps move down in front of you, taking you with them, if you prefer, you can imagine a staircase or an elevator instead. If you have any difficulty visualizing the escalator or staircase or elevator just the count itself will take you deeper and deeper.

(slowly) Ten, now you step on and start going down, nine, eight, seven, six, going deeper and deeper with each count. Five, four, three, still deeper, two one, and zero. Now you step off at the bottom and you will continue to go deeper still with each breath you take, deeper and deeper with each breath. You are so relaxed and so comfortable. Let go still more, notice your breathing, probably it is now slower and you are breathing more from the bottom of your lungs, abdominal breathing, as you go deeper into hypnosis, my voice may seem to drift away from you as though it were coming from a great distance, but you shall continue to hear it and pay attention to the suggestions I shall make to you. You will be able to respond to these suggestions even though you are very relaxed and very comfortable.

Now you can imagine yourself strolling down the hall to a special room. A special room in your own mind as you see yourself strolling down the hall, feeling fine, feeling pleasant and relaxed, you can indicate to yourself when you reach the room, you can have it any way you wish it to be. It can be large or small, light or dark, cool or warm, furnished in any way you wish so that it is pleasant, comfortable and attractive. Now, approaching the door to this special room now seeing yourself opening the door, entering the room, and closing the door. You can arrange yourself in any position that is comfortable, sitting, lying down, or strolling about. As you see yourself in this situation, you can allow yourself to go deeper and deeper, into a very deep state of concentration, a very deep state of relaxation. You know that you can always return to this special room in your mind when you wish to do so. You will be able to learn to use these techniques and these procedures for your own benefit and your own welfare, so that you can learn to relax and rest more deeply, study and concentrate more deeply, and to gain more self-understanding and more self control.

As you continue to use self hypnosis, you are going to gain more self confidence in your ability to accomplish your purposes. You will find that you are able to follow the suggestions you make to yourself in the trance state. You will find yourself able to go more quickly into the trance state whenever you wish to do so. To go into a hynotic trance all you have to do is close your eyes, make yourself comfortable and drift into a state of trance. Sometimes it may help to think to yourself the phrase; "Now I'm going into hypnosis. Repeat to yourself the words, "Relax deeply, relax deeply, relax deeply, thinking these thoughts to yourself silently and slowly. As you do this you will slip into a very comfortable state of trance. You need to say nothing aloud, you merely think these words. When you have down this just take a deep breath and let it out slowly to help you relax and focus on the relaxation just you had done before. Tell your muscles to relax as I have told them before.

When you have finally relaxed your arms, imagine the escalator, think of the escalator or staircase. Now you should count backwards from ten to zero, count very slowly. Whenever you are ready to awaken all you need to do is think to yourself, "Now I'm going to wake up". Then count slowly slowly to five and you will be wide awake. You will always awaken refreshed, relaxed, and feeling fine.

While you are in a hypnotic trance, if anything should happen that you need to react to you will do instantly and spontaneously. Something such as a phone call or a real emergency like a fire, you will awaken instantly and be alert and wide awake. Actually this would happen without a suggestion being necessary because your subconscious mind will always protect you from harm.

Self Hypnosis Sample Script

Now let yourself drift even deeper and deeper into the trance. Just pay attention to your breathing, notice how deep and regular your breathing is, you can go deeper into hypnosis with each breath you take, let each breath carry you deeper and deeper and deeper. Just like going to sleep except that you will keep hearing my voice and following my instructions. Now, continue to go deeper into hypnosis, to become more and more comfortable with each breath that you take. Breathing rhythmically and. deeply, going deeper with each breath, let yourself go completely now, deeper and deeper, now that you are deeply relaxed, I want you to remain that way for a few minutes while you have an interesting and pleasant experience. I will not tell you what to experience, you can have the kind of experience that you choose to have, it may be a surprise to you, it may be a feeling or a memory, or a thought, you just let yourself experience it and enjoy it. As you have this experience you can go deeper and deeper into hypnosis. Now take a few minutes to let yourself experience whatever happens, (three to four minute pause). In a few moments you will be able to complete the thought, feeling or memory. Now imagine that you. are standing at the top of an escalator again. See the steps moving down in front of you, and see the railings. I am going to count from ten to zero, as I start to count, imagine that you are stepping on to the escalator, standing there with your hands on the railings while the steps move down in front of you, taking you with them. Ten, now you step on and start going down. Nine, eight, seven, six, going deeper and deeper with each count, five, four, three, still deeper, two, one, and zero. Now you step off at the bottom and will continue to go deeper and deeper with each breath you take, deeper and deeper with each breath, you are so relaxed and so comfortable. Let go still more. Now I want you to make a suggestion to yourself that you want to carry out. You can stay in a trance while you decide what suggestion you want to make, deciding will be easy, it also will be easy for you to follow the suggestion whenever you wish to complete it. Go ahead now, and make your suggestion. Take whatever time you need, and after you have made your suggestion, you may arouse yourself from the trance at any time you wish and be wide-awake and alert. You will be able to practice these techniques whenever you wish to do so, and you can learn to use them for your own benefit and your own welfare, so that you can become the kind of person you wish to be, the kind of person you can be.

Tests for Self Hypnosis

To recognize whether you are self-hypnotized, and if so, to what depth, you may give yourself a number of tests. It is best not to attempt giving any test to yourself or attempt to produce any hypnotic phenomena until you have practiced self-hypnosis successfully several times. However, when you are sure of achieving the state of self-hypnosis, then you can give relevant tests to yourself. If you respond properly to the tests, then you know you are self-hypnotized. Tests of self-hypnosis are very similar to the hetro-hypnotic depth tests. The only difference between self-hypnosis tests and hetro-hypnosis depth tests is that in the latter the hypnotist gives you the tests, but in the former, the tests are self managed.

Eye Catalepsy Test

After having achieved relaxation and eye closure, suggest to yourself that your eyelids are getting very heavy an they are locked together. You may word your suggestion like this: ONE, my eyes are locked together. TWO, My eyelids are actually so glued that it will be an enormous task to move them. THREE, they are stuck fast, tight, very tight. As you mention the word tight, preferably mentally, try to open them, but stop trying as soon as you are unable to do so. When you respond in satisfactory manner to the test suggestion, give yourself the following suggestion and continue on with the induction procedure: Now my eyes are perfectly normal in every way, and I can open them whenever I choose, but I will keep them closed for remainder of the induction. I am now going even deeper into self-hypnosis. If you respond properly to this test then you can be sure that you are hypnotized.

Arm Catalepsy Test

Levitate one of your hands and suggest to yourself that it is getting rigid and taut, and you cannot bring it down again. After you respond successfully to this test, suggest to yourself that your arm has become loose and limp and is going to drop to your thigh. Include in your suggestion the idea that when your hand touches your thigh you will go to an even deeper state of hypnosis. Another variation of this test is that you suggest to yourself that your hand is getting very heavy, that it is stuck to the arm of the chair, and that you can not move it or lift it up.

Hand Levitation Test

Imagine that one of your hands is beginning to lose all sensation of weight, and it is becoming buoyant. At the count of three, your rising fingers will touch your face (Suggest to yourself that this will be done involuntarily and without conscious effort). After your fingers have touched your face, let your arm drop on your lap and imagine that upon dropping your hand on your thigh, you will develop a much deeper state of hypnosis.

Foot Test

The test can be accomplished while sitting or lying down. First you imagine that one of your feet is very heavy. You imagine that your foot is so heavy that it is stuck to the floor and you are unable to move it or raise it. The harder you try to raise your foot, the less you will be able to do it, until you reach a certain count.

Glove Anesthesia Test

You can give glove anesthesia suggestions to yourself. To produce glove anesthesia you should rub the back of one of your hands clockwise or counter clockwise, and suggest to yourself that by rubbing your hand it becomes numb, senseless, and wooden-like. You will lose all sensation in that hand and you will feel no pain if the hand is stimulated. You may also suggest to yourself that numbness will develop in your hand simultaneously with hand levitation, and will remain in your hand until a certain period of time after awakening. Wording of the suggestion should be something like this; upon awakening, my hand will be numb, cold and senseless for one minute. When anesthesia is affected in your hand, you will feel a little pressure on the spot that you choose to pinch, but no pain.

If you succeed in passing these tests, you can be sure that you have developed at least a medium state of hypnosis. As you keep practicing, a greater depth of hypnosis will be produced.

Deep Muscle Relaxation Training

This is the first of a three-phase program to prepare you for Self-Hypnosis. The end result of this session is for you to have a heightened sense of awareness of what it feels like for your body to be relaxed. This technique alone will not teach you every thing you need to know. It is imperative that you practice all three phases of this program. The number of seconds to pause is denoted by the number in parent sis (0).

Script

We will begin with you becoming comfortable. (10) You can either be sitting down in a chair or lying down. If you use a chair, try to make it one with arms, if lying down, do not use a pillow. If your clothing is too tight and uncomfortable, loosen it slightly now (4). Settle back now as comfortable as you can (4). Focus your attention on my voice (3). As other thoughts drift into your mind, let them drift away and continue to focus on my voice only (4). (Spend four minutes talking the client through a deep breathing exercise,). As you relax, clench your right fist, now clench your fist tighter and tighter, and study the tension in your feelings of tension (5,). Now straighten out your arms (4.). Let them relax, and now feel the difference again (13). Let the relaxation develop (8.). Once more, tense your biceps (.4.). Hold that tension and observe it carefully (4.). Straighten your arms and allow the feelings of relaxation to flow into yours arms (4). Relax to the best of your ability (8). Now straighten your arms so that you feel the most tension in the triceps muscle along the back of your arms (3). Now relax (5.). Move your arms back into a comfortable position (5). Let the relaxation flow on its own accord (8). Your arms should feel- comfortably heavy as you allow the relaxation to flow (5). Once more, straighten your arms so that you feel the tension in your triceps (8). Let your arms relax again and focus on the comfortable heavy feeling of relaxation in your arms (6). Now let's focus on pure relaxation in the arms without any tension. Move your arms into a comfortable position and let them relax (8). Let the relaxation flow into your arms (3). Focus on that nice warm feeling in your arms (10). Even when your arms seem fully relaxed, try to let your arms achieve a deeper level of relaxation (12). Now we will move upwards to the head and shoulders (2). We will start by letting all your muscles go loose and heavy. Just settle back quietly and comfortably. Wrinkle up your forehead now (3). Wrinkle it tighter (5). Now stop wrinkling your forehead (4). Relax and allow it to smooth out (31). Picture your entire forehead and scalp becoming smoother as the relaxation continues to build (10). You can notice the tree as a leaf starts to fall. Just starting its fall (10). The warm breeze is cradling the leaf (10). Rocking the leaf gently back and forth (10). The leaf moves ever so slowly in the breeze (10). Feel that warm gentle breeze again, gently touching your face (10). Notice the free flowing relaxation going through your body (15). You also notice that the leaf is still falling ever so slowly (10). It is still being cradled and rocked, back and forth by the gentle warm breeze you feel. (15). The leaf is still slowly working its way down in its descent to the ground

(15). The leaf is moving so slowly-y and unhurried. (15). Still gently floating and moving so gracefully with the breeze (15). Unhurried or bothered by time, the leaf continues its slow and deliberate descent to the ground (15). Let your mind slowly turn inward to become re-aware of the wonderful state of relaxation your body is enjoying (20). That comfortable, warm heavy feeling continues to flow throughout your person (30). Now your mind slowly turns back to the leaf (5). It is still moving so graceful. descent downward. still gently swaying in the breeze (10). Back and forth, so slowly and gently, as it moves to its downward destination (15). With slow graceful. motion, the warm pleasant breeze you feel is still- carrying the leaf further downward (15). You observe the leaf moving with gentle and tender grace (15.). The leaf is being cradled by the warm breeze, you can also feel the comfort at any time you wish and be wide-awake and alert. You will be able to practice these techniques whenever you wish to do so, and you can learn to use them for your own benefit and your own welfare, so that you can become the kind of person you wish to be...the kind of person you can be.

About the Author

Randy Hartman has a masters degree in Human Relations from the University of Oklahoma. He has been a Clinical Hypnotherapist and trainer for more than 25 years. Randy has written a total of five books on the subject of hypnosis.